Mind Mapping to Success

How to Use Visual Maps to Solve Problems & Hack Productivity, Time Management, and Creativity for Business & Daily Life

Written by Charlotte C.M.

© Copyright Charlotte C.M. 2019 - All rights reserved.

The content contained within this book may not be reproduced, duplicated or transmitted without direct written permission from the author or the publisher.

Under no circumstances will any blame or legal responsibility be held against the publisher, or author, for any damages, reparation, or monetary loss due to the information contained within this book. Either directly or indirectly.

Legal Notice:

This book is copyright protected. This book is only for personal use. You cannot amend, distribute, sell, use, quote or paraphrase any part, or the content within this book, without the consent of the author or publisher.

Disclaimer Notice:

Please note the information contained within this document is for educational and entertainment purposes only. All effort has been executed to present accurate, up to date, and reliable, complete information. No warranties of any kind are declared or implied. Readers acknowledge that the author is not engaging in the rendering of legal, financial, medical or professional advice. The content within this book has been derived from various sources. Please consult a licensed professional before attempting any techniques outlined in this book.

By reading this document, the reader agrees that under no circumstances is the author responsible for any losses, direct or indirect, which are incurred as a result of the use of information contained within this document, including, but not limited to, — errors, omissions, or inaccuracies.

"The secret of making dreams come true can be summarized in four C's. They are Curiosity, Confidence, Courage, and Constancy; and the greatest of these is Confidence."

—*Walt Disney*

Just for you!

A FREE GIFT TO OUR READERS

20 ready-to-use templates that you can download and start mind mapping with right away! Visit this link:

www.thisischarlotte.com/mindmapping

Table of Contents

Table of Contents	iii
Preface	ix
Introduction	1
The Benefits of Mind Maps	4
How People Have Used Mind Maps in History	6
Creating your First Map	9
Before You Begin	10
Your First Mind Map	12
Problems You May Encounter	14
How to Use a Mind Map Effectively	18
When and Why Mind Maps Work?	20
How to Apply a Mind Map to a Situation	21
When Can Mind Maps be Helpful?	22
Where they Might Fall Short?	23
The Science Behind Mind Maps	27
The Brain Architecture and Mind Maps	28
Learning and Caring for the Mind with Mind Maps	31
How Do We Learn?	32
Memory and Repetition	36
Listening	39
How to Make a Mind Map	41
Noting and Brainstorming Ideas	43
Create A Mind Map in Five Steps	45

    Components of a Mind Map   50

Brainstorming with Mind Maps   **55**
    The Rules of Brainstorming   57
    How to Come Up with Ideas (Even If You Don't Have Any)   58
    How to Brainstorm When you Don't Have an End Goal   60

Mind Mapping for Writing   **67**
    How to Write Better   67
    How to Write an Essay   69
    How To Create an Essay Plan   73
    How to Plan-out a Book for Authors   73
    Non-fiction Book Planning   78
    Fiction Book Planning   80

Notetaking with Mind Maps   **84**
    Notetaking, Reading and Studying with Mind Maps   85
    How to Take Notes of Books   87
    How to Take Notes of Speeches or Lectures   90
    How to Create a List   92

Mind Mapping for Planning   **94**
    How to Set Goals   94
    How to Embrace Change   97
    How to Improve Time Management & Organization   102

Mind Mapping for Decision Making   **108**
    How Do We Make Decisions?   109
    Evaluating Choices with Mind Maps   110

Using Mind Maps to Improve Study Methods   **112**
    How to Take Faster Notes with Mind Maps   113
    How to Study Better with Mind Maps   114
    Recommendations: Future Chapters That Will Enhance your Study Skills   117

Mind Mapping for Mindset — 119
- How to Find Purpose — 120
- How to Visualize Your Life Goals — 123
- Crafting your Ideal Future — 124
- Top Tips to when Crafting your Ideal Future: — 126

How to Recall Information — 128
- How to Remember Better — 130
- How to Remember Names — 131
- How to Remember Facts — 137
- How to Remember Lost Items — 139

Mind Mapping for Creativity — 143
- Leadership with Mind Maps — 144
- How to Promote Idea Generation (Free Thinking) and Innovation — 148
- Mind Mapping for Strategic Thinking — 149

Mind Mapping for Business & Work Performance — 153
- Estimating Project Timelines — 154
- Preparing for Negotiations — 156
- How to Create Successful Presentations — 158
- Mind Mapping for Effective Management — 162
- Mind Mapping for Better Sales and Marketing — 163
- Mind Mapping for a Meeting — 166
- Mind Mapping for Interviews — 168

Mind Mapping your Business Idea — 169
- Start with your Business Idea — 170
- How to Form a Business Model Using Mind Maps — 172
- Growing your Business Idea — 176

Mind Mapping for Problem Solving — 179
- How to Find Solutions & Answers — 180
- How to Diagnose Problems — 182

Mind Mapping for Learning New Languages   **186**
    Using Mind Maps for Learning   187
    How to Organize Your Words When Learning a New Language   188
    How to Compare Languages   192

Mind Mapping for Everyday Life   **194**
    Networking   195
    Shopping for Gifts   196
    Planning a Wedding   197
    Meal Planning and Food Shopping List   199
    Health and fitness   200

Mind Mapping with Children   **203**
    Helping Children to Express their Ideas   204
    Why Mind Mapping Works for Children   205
    Make Mind Mapping a Game   206
    Using a Mind Map to Help Children Learn   210
    Using Mind Mapping to Form a Story   213

Group Mind Mapping   **215**
    Group Ideas and Ensuring Everyone Counts   216
    The Benefits of Group Mind Mapping   217
    The Drawbacks of Group Mind Mapping   218
    Good Practices for Group Mind Mapping   219

Mind Mapping Software   **221**
    Free Software to Create Mind Maps   222

Beyond Mind Mapping   **224**
    Concepts that are Similar to Mind Maps   225
    Concise Learning Method (CLM)   226
    Speed Mind Mapping   227
    Conclusion   228

Reference List   **230**

Preface

I'm a DINOSAUR!

And this is its head, and that's the flame. It shoots both fire and ice breath, and it also has lasers coming out of his eyes.

That's how my six-year-old nephew responds when I ask him, "What did you draw?"

When I look at it, all I see is this flea-like creature.

Remember those days when all you needed was a piece of paper, and some coloring pencils, and you could create anything possible just by digging into your imagination. Your creativity was boundless. It was plentiful, unrestricted, *anything was possible*.

You used colors, shapes and lines- three simple things, and suddenly you had mystical unicorn-cats, with rainbow fur that could fly with a magical cloud carpet. Or, the perfect boyfriend, with one green eye and one blue eye, a chiselled body, holding a pack of Reese's in one hand, and flowers in the other.

Creativity was literally exploding out of every part of you.

Now, let's fast-forward a little. When you start to grow up and it's not as cool to be creative and free-thinking anymore.

Trace this letter, and follow the lines!

Color inside the lines, and don't go outside. And this one's blue, not teal.

No, that's not a unicorn, that's just a horse.

Hey, don't doodle in the sides. This notebook is for taking notes.

You can't use markers or crayons to write… That's for children.

What…? You want to DRAW right now? That's what you want to do instead of working? What are you, five?

Time and time again, we get reminded by our peers that it's too much to be creative outside of the age of when it's okay to be. We are prescribed that there are better ways of learning, and the "fun" ways we grew up with are wrong.

If you aren't making a detailed list or chart, or writing out notes, then you aren't learning or brainstorming the right way.

In grade 3, while my friends were learning their multiplication tables with practice and memorization, I was struggling. I would get all the numbers jumbled in my head when I looked at it. The only way I learnt my tables was by singing it through songs. I loved music, and singing, and my parents found me a multiplication tables song, and I listened to them on repeat in the car. Until today, that's how I remember my 7 times table.

In high school, I struggled through my grade 12 advanced physics class. My teacher, didn't believe in real numbers, so replaced everything with variables in a formula.

How the hell am I supposed to learn if I can't even visualize the number and give it context?! It just didn't make sense.

So he taught me to draw diagrams for every single problem. And visualize it myself, because heck, numbers are just symbols that we assigned some sort of meaning to.

In university, I studied engineering, and once again, *I was struggling.* I couldn't remember any of the formulas and how to apply them like my friends did.

I had to create stories that I could relate the formulas too, so I remembered exactly which one to use at which time. I created clouds of information that were linked to one another, so I could see how things worked big picture.

Today, as a product designer, it's my responsibility to make things work. I create products and bring a client's idea to life. They don't give instructions or directions. They give me an end goal, and it's my job to figure out how to get there, without knowing how to get there exactly.

Client: *Can you design me a website that people can understand my product really easily. It also has to be mobile responsive, have a quick load time, and be SEO optimized.*

Me: *Okay, do you know what you want it to look like? Or what content should be optimized?*

Client: *Oh, I don't know. You figure it out.*

I had to learn to see the full vision, without even knowing what the vision was.

So what do you do? You need to think outside the box. You need to get creative and think about all the possible factors that might affect a design. And in the design world, we are visual thinkers. Everything comes back to brainstorming and coming up with ideas.

You draw everything out. You look at what's on paper, you write out ideas, you create simple prototypes, and force yourself to think with ingenuity.

With a combination of my design thinking, and the methodologies taught in engineering, I discovered a unique approach to problem solving. In engineering, we are taught that every little thing is connected to one another. This is called "The System's Approach". Every idea is a moving part, like a cog in a gear, powering a bigger motor.

By combining analytical thinking, and visualization, problem solving was becoming easier and easier.

Over the years I've found success in my career as a designer, and even in everyday life because I was able to think radially, color outside the lines, and consider things as part of a bigger system.

I thought to myself, *how can I show others how to think bigger than what they currently do, in any situation?*

Cue, mind maps.

In 2011, I began to use mind maps regularly for just about any situation. Creating my grocery list for the week, prioritizing tasks at work, setting my goals for the new year, qualities to find in a partner, you name it. I was astonished by their power and flexibility, and how you could do it on your phone or even the back of a napkin (definitely not the fanciest approach, but sometimes you're desperate!)

Mind maps aren't a new concept. It's based on visual decision making, which has been around for decades. But, no one writes books about it, unless you start giving things fancy names and labels- then boom, everyone wants to try it.

I made this book so other people can get their shit together, with a super simple-to-follow method, where you don't have to pay $1,000 to attend some life changing seminar to unlock secrets to your success.

I hope you start using mind maps to their full potential. Some of you may have tried in the past, but many do not know the basics, or have not mastered the concepts or utilized the tools, styles and formats available to them. Even a beginner can start with this book and learn how to produce visual maps for various situations.

Assuming we are all human here, in the upcoming chapters, I discuss the way we think, process, store and recall information using our brain and memory.

I want to show you the power we can tap into by utilizing mind mapping techniques. You'll discover how to create and apply mind maps, and how to exploit them to carve your path to success in almost any real-world application. Whether you are a student struggling to pass exams, an author with writer's block, a bride-to-be planning her own wedding, someone trying to learn a new language, or simply trying to plan a grocery list, this book is perfect for you.

The world is fast-paced and in order to succeed in education, work, or life, we must be forward-thinking, creative and innovative. Mind maps can help us to be all three. This book will show that mind mapping techniques offer something for everyone, regardless of learning style, age, and preference. It will start with the basics and show how simple it is to create a visual map, but it will also demonstrate different styles and formats that help us to thrive as people and in business.

Mind maps will give us the edge we need to grow and stay one step ahead. Open your mind and read on. It's time to stand out from the crowd in business, in education and as an individual!

Introduction

A mind map is a useful and creative planning tool used to explore ideas and concepts. It is an effective way of transferring ideas and concepts from your brain, onto a page. Images and colors can be used to enhance your thought process and prompt your memory. You form your ideas using a tree or spider-like diagram to display your thoughts and ideas visually in relation to a specific topic or subject. For example, what do you think about when I say apple?

Some people might think of the fruit, while others may think of technology-based items created by Apple Inc. It may even prompt you to think of the old saying *'An apple each day, keeps the doctor away.'*

The diagrams, images and words used in a mind map encourage you to think and record any ideas or thoughts you have onto paper in an efficient, but visual way. You can then develop your ideas or concepts based on this and like any map, you can plan your journey to achieving your end goal, from start to finish.

When you first start writing a mind map, you are simply aiming to record every idea you have in relation to a specific topic or subject. If you are planning a strategy for instance, you could make several mind maps. First, you would detail everything you want to include in one diagram as this would help you to develop the strategy, and then you would plan how you would write this. You might even create a mind map summing up why this new strategy is needed, by reflecting on the benefits and drawbacks. Your initial draft is a collection of thoughts and ideas, so don't worry if this is not in order. Mind maps are often the first stage of planning and are designed to provide you with the foundations you need to grow your idea.

Once your ideas are on the page, you can start organizing and structuring your mind map by putting it in order, exploring the pros and cons of each sub-topic. For each sub-topic, you can note any additional information or expand on each of your ideas. You could even create smaller mind maps to help you analyze each of the sub-topic areas and what they entail.

Mind maps can be the start of something great!

The Benefits of Mind Maps

There are many benefits of using these visual maps, as they appeal to many learning styles. An image can help us to remember, recall and process information easily. According to Hayes, 'One of the best-known methods of representing information is a sensory image, such as sounds or pictures.' [1] Some of these benefits are detailed below:

1. Mind maps allow us to think creatively without forcing the thought process, as they look at getting those thoughts and ideas on a page for you to reflect on later. When you start to remove the ideas from your head, you can start to emphasize ways of developing those ideas and concepts further.

2. They are great for getting us to focus on a specific idea or concept, as this is detailed at the center of the diagram, so you are always reminded of the specific point. This means you are less likely to stray from your topic.

3. Mind maps are quick and concise. If you have a central idea or concept, mind mapping can be a quick and concise way to map out your thoughts and journey. You cannot add too

many details, but you can consider the advantages and disadvantages of your sub-topics quickly, without exploring them in an in-depth way. You can empty the ideas from your brain at a fast, effective rate. Once they are on paper, your mind feels at ease and you can consider and organize your thoughts rationally.

4. Visual representations appeal to different learning styles, which means we can process information effectively and efficiently, as well as remember it. Hayes mentions that imagery prompts us to remember as we can use images and colors in the diagram. This helps us to memorize information or create a mental image using key words.

5. Mind maps encourage radiant thinking. Tony Buzan calls the way that the brain generates its ideas, based on one central concept *Radiant Thinking*. He suggests that our thoughts "radiate" in several directions and we can have several thoughts and ideas at once as the brain is non-linear. One idea can prompt many, because of the way we think. [2]

How People Have Used Mind Maps in History

Images and visual maps or aids have been used over hundreds of years, so creative thinking is not a new concept. Over time, mind maps have gained momentum because they help people learn and are great for prompting memory. Many educational establishments like schools, colleges and universities, embed mind mapping techniques when they teach study skills and their lecturers incorporate them into their lesson planning. They are flexible tools with many uses, for example, writers often use them to grow their creative ideas. This means that mind maps could have been used when your favorite novel or TV show was being planned, in the very early stages.

It is believed that philosopher, Porphyry of Tyros, was the first to adopt mind mapping concepts, to express ideas in the 3rd Century. Porphyry used the as a tool to break down philosophical ideas and concepts, as he wanted to improve learning. His notable works include, *Introduction to Categories* and this comments on the *Categories of Aristotle*. He focused on logic and made it easier to educate others by improving their learning experience, using visual aids. [3]

Ramon Llull, a famous Catalan Philosopher, is also said to have utilized such concepts. When writing his most famous works, *Catalan Literature,* he used mind mapping to brainstorm his ideas, and also as a comparative tool, to compare different religions. He often used visual aids to persuade, and in one of his later works, he designed a 'machine'. This was basically a logic-based diagram and his aim was to persuade Muslims to become Christians based on this comparative tool. [4]

Leonardo da Vinci is another notable figure in history, known to have used mind mapping concepts. He often drew them when notetaking and today, this remains a popular notetaking method.

Mind mapping gained attention during the 1950s. Dr Alan Collins used mind maps to develop basic learning theories in the 1960s and it became much more modern at this stage, as mapping increased in creativity. Tony Buzan, a British Psychologist developed a set of rules for mind mapping, and this was a turning point as he explored and tested their limits by applying them to a variety of situations.[5]

Over time, we have become so much better at using mind maps. Major corporations, like Apple, create and develop their visions and ideas by using mind mapping techniques because of their flexibility. We can use them in groups to come up with business ideas. We can use them when planning our writing, stories, or an essay. They can also be used for planning projects and strategies too. Software has been developed to help with our mind mapping to meet the needs of people who are not confident creating visuals on paper, or for businesses who want a more professional look. We will look at several free mind mapping software later in this book.

Just remember that one spectacular concept or idea can be developed with a mind map, and this can result in a multi-million-dollar business and the world at your feet. Anything is possible with mind maps!

1

Creating your First Map

In this chapter, we are preparing you for your first mind map. If you've never created a mind map before, this chapter will be useful as it will make sure you know what you are trying to achieve and the types of issues that you may come across. Now, there are some things you should know before you start, so make sure you read on, even if you are familiar with mind maps.

Before You Begin

Creating a mind map is not something you should do in every situation. If we understand them, it becomes easier to decide if should or should not create one. If you want to create a mind map successfully, there are some things you need to know first:

You must know your central idea, concept, topic or thought and ideally, you should know this before you begin. If you are thinking about creating a mind map, you need to have a central idea, concept or goal. Without this, you will have no basis for your mind map as your central idea is your starting point.

You need to know the end goal or purpose. You need to have a direction or purpose for your mind map, so it is important to know the purpose of your map. Ask yourself 'What do I want to achieve?' You may have a new business idea, want to write a novel, or you may even want to plan an essay. Regardless of your reasons, a mind map is a great way to start exploring your ideas or concepts.

Be prepared to be surprised. The mind is a funny thing and it does not always take us in the direction we expect. The whole idea of a mind map is to encourage free and radiant thinking, so when you first start to write your mind map, you might find that ideas spring to mind from your subconscious that you have never really considered. This is a good thing! *Radiant Thinking* starts with a central idea, problem or concept that prompts further ideas in response. It represents how the brain is prompted visually to think and how thoughts and ideas can stem from this central idea. For example, if your central idea is a problem, let's say we live in Paris and need to travel to London, we could explore different possible travel methods that could get us from Paris to London. We know that we can travel by train, boat or ferry, car, or flights and this would then prompt us to evaluate these methods further for instance, we might consider costs, comfort and speed of each method. A visual map would help us decide what travel method to choose for our journey, and all of this was prompted by a central problem; getting from one place to another.

A mind map does not need to be neat. The first draft of your mind map will not be neat. This early planning stage is often used to generate ideas. As mentioned earlier, it is about getting your ideas from your brain, down onto the paper. Once you have emptied your mind of your initial ideas, you can always reflect and analyze later. You may decide to remove or add further viable ideas or concepts as you go, which is fine too. Make your diagram work for you!

Your First Mind Map

Your first map will be an array of ideas, so you can think freely and creatively. It should be flexible, so you can swap things around and change its order. When you see the words or images on the page, it will be easier to organize your thoughts. If you use your mind map effectively, it can prompt you, help you explore the pros and cons of ideas and concepts, and assist you when planning and strategizing. Mind maps encourage creative thinking, meaning that your ideas and concepts can lead you in different directions. This tool is incredibly powerful for sparking further inspiration and innovation.

When you create your first mind map, make sure you formulate a central idea or concept that you want to explore, allow yourself to think freely and get as much down on the paper as possible. You should write your central idea in the center of the page and then draw soft lines or branches from this idea, linking to sub-topic ideas. You can also develop a color code and use images too.

CAREER GOALS

- Art Teacher
  - Children
  - Adults
- Artist
- Art Expert
- Qualifications Degree
  - Art & Design
  - Fine Art
  - Art History
- Experience
  - Volunteer
  - Competitions
  - Art Gallery
  - Teaching
- Transferrable Skills
  - Patience
  - Organised
  - Demonstrating
  - Communication
  - Professional

Mind maps are powerful images that can help us to memorize and develop our ideas, but you *must* have an idea and concept to work from to start. This is not a magic tool, but it can help you plan, organize and process your own thoughts, ideas and concepts while prompting us to improve, develop and strategize. There are so many uses, as they are useful for notetaking, business planning, story planning, planning your writing, decision making and so much more. If you follow this book and use them effectively, you can expect great things.

Problems You May Encounter

Mind maps may not be ideal for everyone or every situation. Here are some of the most common problems you may encounter:

I'm not good at drawing. Now, we have seen some very pretty, organized and colorful mind maps, but you do not have to be an artist or designer to produce this. If you prefer you can make yours simple, or you can use online pictures and images (subject to copyright laws) when producing your map. Color coding is a great way to organize your map, without actually drawing. You can also use an online mind mapping software.

I want a perfect mind map. Many people expect to produce a perfect mind map instantly and this is not always the case when you produce a hand-drawn or written diagram. Mind mapping software can also be limiting, as you have limited control over the design. Your mind map is a creative tool and it is never going to be perfect on your first attempt. If you want a perfect mind map, you must work on it and refine it. Do not expect a perfect mind map on your first attempt because you could set yourself up for disappointment.

How should I develop my idea? Sometimes we have an initial idea or concept, but we then are unsure of how to proceed. Start by noting down some simple and obvious ideas and try to allow the thought process to happen naturally. Stick to visual symbols, pictures and key words and try to link related subjects together. You can also put connecting lines between ideas and remember, this is your creative map so adopt a personal style of your own.

A mind map limits my ideas as it lacks detail. A common issue or roadblock is that you do not have much space to write down your idea. Mind maps are meant to be concise, so you are not meant to write down lots of information at this stage, but this can be used to your advantage. You can narrow down your idea or concept based on this. Training your brain to write less is trickier than writing more. If you go on to write a plan or a strategy, then you will be able to expand your ideas, but at the initial planning stage, less is more. Imagine writing lots of information about a specific product or service you want to launch, only to then find out that you prefer another product or service. Mind maps can help us figure out what ideas and concepts will work, before we explore in-depth. Say you brainstorm new products and services for your business, you would then end up with a list of

15

products and services. At this point you can write the pros and cons of your product or service ideas. You can then choose from your list which product or service will be best for your business. Then you would choose a product or service and create a separate mind map exploring this. Mind maps are not limiting as such, they just help you to break down your ideas into small chunks by focusing on one area. They help you narrow down a big idea or ideas, into their simplest form.

I'm struggling to organize my map. Another common problem is how to arrange and structure your ideas and concepts. If you have a niche process or strategy, and your mind map includes many ideas and thoughts, you then need to organize this in a logical order. For some people, this happens easily, but for others, it can be difficult. This depends on the way we learn and process information personally. This book will explore different ways of organizing your mind map and compare the different ways that we learn and process information. This will help you understand the techniques used in visual maps and how to use them effectively.

I find mind maps repetitive. Another common problem is the repetitiveness of a mind map. They are not designed to be repetitive, but they do rely on your brain to think of ideas and concepts. If you find you repeat information, maybe you need to take a moment and think as you may need to change your approach or do some further research. For example, if you want to create one new product and you have an initial idea, your mind map should not discuss products you want to create for your business because you already have an idea. Trying to think of other products at this stage could confuse things, so the best thing here is to focus on your current thoughts and consider who your product is for (customer), what your product is, when you want the product to be finished/launched, and why this product is appealing to your audience (why will it solve their problems). If you decide that this product is not suitable, you could then change your approach (once your initial idea is expelled from your brain and on paper). For example, you may wish to consider other products that your business could produce instead. Maybe you need to research what your competitors are doing and the market trends of your ideal client, as this may spark some further ideas. Remember you should never copy others, but you should use your creative skills to produce your own, unique thing.

How to Use a Mind Map Effectively

If you want to use an effective visual map, keep it as simple as possible. The mind map provides you a space to detail your thoughts, without overwhelming you.

When you first create your diagram, it may be best to start with a brainstorm-style map if you don't have a specific topic in mind. For example, if I wanted to start a business, then I might brainstorm all the different products and services I can offer, because the main thing here is to get every business product and service we can offer, down on paper. If we were writing an essay, we would already have a research question and therefore, our mind map is niched to that and it can be discussed further. The brainstorm style is much more a starting point whereas the niched mind map, is the next stage.

Think about your end goal and use the information in your diagram to organize your thoughts. Think about how your ideas will help you attain this, after all, your mind map is your journey to achieving your end goal. Formulate questions based on your images, key words and ideas – think about who, what, when, where, how and why.

According to a study by Cain (2001/2002), mind maps can help improve concentration, questioning techniques and they also promote independence. [6] Refining these skills can help in many aspects in our life. It can alter the way we plan, prepare, structure and organize our thoughts, concepts and ideas in the future. In later chapters of this book, we will explore different ways of applying the mind map, to various scenarios.

2

When and Why Mind Maps Work?

It is important to know when and why mind maps work, so that we know when we can apply or use them. Once we know this, we can start to examine why mind maps work by reviewing the science behind them. This will give us a greater understanding of how our brain works and thinks when it comes to visual maps and representations.

How to Apply a Mind Map to a Situation

As mentioned earlier in chapter 1, it is important to understand the purpose of your mind map, as this will influence the way you apply it to a situation. Visuals are a great way of provoking creative thinking and they are also a good way to analyze situations, form plans and build strategies.

The next stage is to apply it to a situation, but this is dependent on the purpose of your mind map. If you are creating this when notetaking, you can use different colors and sub-headings to separate your ideas. If you are creating a story or novel, then you might plan the different steps in the plot, note any key events and link into characters and setting.

Once your map is complete, you can start to explore your initial ideas and expand on them, by concentrating on each sub-topic. Read through your points and think about how they relate to the central idea.

When applying your mind map, it is important to use the questioning techniques we mentioned in chapter 1: who, what, when, where, why and how, to examine your ideas further. If you have several ideas, ensure you review the pros and cons of each.

At this stage, you should be referring to your central idea and consider whether you are on target. Use your thoughts and ideas to map out your journey to achieving your end goal and think about what stage you are currently at. *Are you making progress?*

There are many approaches to mind mapping, and this is because there are many different types and styles. For example, notetaking styles are unlike the visual mapping of a story or business model as each will take on their own form and shape. We will explore the different approaches to creating and applying the mind map, by reviewing different scenarios, in each chapter of this book. No style is right or wrong, because it's for you to create and interpret. Their design should work for you, as they are unique for each person.

When Can Mind Maps be Helpful?

We have already discussed the benefits of mind mapping in general, but there are many benefits as an individual too. It is an effective way of getting information from your brain, as it's a visual diagram. We already know that this can aid us when organizing our thoughts, planning projects and strategies, and it can also help us to analyze ideas and concepts, but how can this really help us?

- To start with, visual images are used to prompt memory, because studies show they are effective.
- They can help us to focus.
- They are concise and clear.
- They are multipurpose, as we can use them in many situations or scenarios.
- In most cases, they can be produced quickly. This depends on whether there is a strong central idea.
- They can help you to put things into perspective.
- They are simple to use.
- They provide us with a foundation for further exploration, which gives us direction.

Where they Might Fall Short?

It would be wrong to suggest that mind maps are for everyone or can be used in any situation. Although there are many benefits, there are some obvious disadvantages too.

- **A mind map has no determined structure.** Structure is created, rather than being provided, which can cause a problem for people who prefer to think in a linear way.
- **They are not as appealing to an auditory learner,** as they rely on imagery and appeal to visual and spatial learners. As you have to create them yourself, they can appeal to kinesthetic learners, especially if you construct them by using images or sticky notes. Sticky notes allow flexibility, so you can alter your thought process and its structure effectively, to suit your needs.
- **Everyone processes information differently and if you like to read detailed information, listen or talk through notions, then a mind map may not be the best way for you to learn or investigate ideas**. Mind maps do not suit every scenario, but they are flexible and can be adapted depending on your learning preferences. You could be brief in the early stages but if you feel you need more detail, there is nothing stopping you in taking a sub-topic and creating a mind map solely on that topic. This will give you the opportunity to research and add more detail.
- **They limit information.** A common disadvantage of a mind map is that it limits information. This is an advantage to some people, but a disadvantage to others. If you are

mapping out a process, then limiting information is a positive thing, as process maps are used to break down ideas. They work best when they are divided into simple and clear steps that are easy to follow. Obviously, if you are writing a whole strategy or story, then details may be required, so you would then use your mind map as an outline, and then fill in the gaps extensively with the details as you produce your end product.

- **You need to trust your intuitive side, rather than the logical.** If you are a linear or logical thinker, mind mapping could be difficult for you. You must use your intuition and be willing to note down all your ideas to empty your brain, and some individuals do not have trust or confidence in their intuitive side.
- **It takes too much time.** Again, this is a common disadvantage for some, others would argue that a mind map is concise and quick. Until you have tried and practiced, you may not know if it is a fast or slow method for you as this depends on the individual. This really depends on you and the strength of your central idea or concept. If you have a topic but are struggling to expand on this through mind mapping, maybe you need to consider this further by researching your options. This could spark further inspiration.

- **Mind mapping is not always practical.** It is not a magical concept that can be used for every situation. Sometimes a simple list will do, or maybe you could just write down your idea with some pointers in a notebook. If you want to mind map, there is a time and a place. To start with, you must have the tools you need to create this, and this could depend on your location at the time. For example, if you are on a holiday and have a sudden novel, you may not have a notebook or laptop to hand. In this case it would not be practical, so you may decide to record your idea on your mobile phone. In order to mind map effectively, you must choose an appropriate time, place and topic.

Mind maps are excellent for solving problems too, as whenever there is a problem (or disadvantage) there is a solution. If you are still unsure, you can use this book to explore the different types or scenarios used for mind mapping. You can then create your own, unique visual map as you will be guided through the process.

The Science Behind Mind Maps

A mind map is a visual map of our thoughts and ideas. The brain processes symbols, images, and colors in a unique way and for most people, it means that we remember, and store information presented to us in this way, easily.

The brain is not a straightforward system as it works in a non-linear way. When we receive information to the brain, we automatically make connections. This is because the brain thinks in a creative way and it 'radiates' many thoughts and ideas, based around a central idea or concept. It is natural for the brain to make sense of information as it processes logical, colorful images. [7]

Tony Buzan coined the term 'radiant thinking' and suggests that there are five major functions. They are receiving, holding, analyzing, outputting, and controlling. He says that the brain receives information from any one of our senses and our memory holds this. The brain then remembers patterns and processes the information it has received. The brain then thinks and communicates the information. The controlling function is how we use this information to form our health and attitude. Basically, this is any mental or physical function, and it's programmed to ensure that the brain reacts in the most effective way possible. [8]

Visual diagrams appeal to our memory because of the way that our brain works and processes information. Symbols and pictures have been used to communicate and tell stories for thousands of years because they are memorable. A mind map appeals to all five major brain functions mentioned above by Buzan, and therefore encourages us to use our brain's full potential. This means we are encouraged to think creatively and expand our thoughts further.

The Brain Architecture and Mind Maps

The brain is made up of the right and left hemispheres and both sides function differently as they are dominant in different areas. The left hemisphere appears to be dominant in a range of mental skills, while the right is more dominant on intellectual skills, like the imagination. Some experts suggest that we can learn to access both sides effectively.

The brain is made up of braincells and every time we have a thought or relive a memory, a biochemical electromagnetic pathway is formed. This pathway is known as the memory trace and the more times you repeat this, the more likely you are to embed this into your mind. This is known as a mental map.

Dr. Roger Sperry completed some very innovative research into the Cerebral Hemisphere, which refers to the right and left hemisphere collectively. Sperry's research focused on intellectual tasks (which he called cortical skills), and he noticed specific benefits. He suggests that the brain's performance improved when mind mapping was used as all cortical skills are utilized. It also enhanced memory power because of the way the brain processes imagery. [9]

Mind mapping appeals to both sides of the brain because both mental skills and intellectual skills are used. Our brain is attracted to colors, images and symbols, and it automatically organizes them in a logical way. Of course, you can learn from written information too, but as Tony Buzan points out, we can lose our concentration easily, if we are presented with lots of written information.

A visual map itself mirrors the brain and the idea of radiant thinking. This is because the brain is at the center of all our ideas and concepts. Through creative thinking, our thoughts expand and radiate from this, often randomly. Our logic then puts them in order. This is very similar to how our brain operates and although a mind map can appear messy at first, they are a great visual aid. We discussed the benefits of using mind maps in chapter 1, but now we know more about how the brain works, we can begin to understand why these techniques are successful. Our brain likes to make sense of the information and ideas it processes and stores, as this is how we learn. In the next chapter, we will think about how mind mapping helps us to learn.

3

Learning and Caring for the Mind with Mind Maps

As human beings, we all have needs and they can be either physical or mental. Caring for our mind is important to stay healthy. As we discussed in the previous chapter, this can impact how we process information, ideas and thoughts. If we are stressed or tired, then we are unlikely to process information in the same way as we would if were refreshed and happy. It is important to keep our mind active, to ensure it stays healthy and alert. It is only then that we can learn new things.

How Do We Learn?

Learning keeps our mind active and it can improve our mental health. We all learn in different ways and this can depend on our own personal preferences, or our preferred way of processing information. Some people learn well through images and diagrams, while others learn with a more hands-on approach, or by reading or listening information. Often, people prefer a combination of learning styles.

American Psychologist, Howard Gardner, researched intelligence and wrote, *Frames of the Mind: The Theory of Multiple Intelligences.* This is useful if we want to start to understand the different ways that ourselves and others, learn. Gardner suggests that there are 9 intelligences and prior to his claim, other scientists had referred to these as soft skills. Gardner realized there was so much more to be said because they influence the way we learn. He suggests that people may falter in one area but excel in another. He said that this does not necessarily determine whether we are smart but demonstrates that we see things from different perspectives. [10]

The 9 Types of Intelligence

THE TYPES OF
INTELLIGENCE

Frames of Mind:
The Theory of Multiple
Intelligences

by Howard Gardner

intra-personal	understanding yourself, what you feel, and what you want
linguistic	finding the right words to express what you mean
kinesthetic	coordinating your mind with your body
interpersonal	sensing people's feelings and motives
existential	tackling the questions of why we live and why we die
logical-mathematical	qualifying things, making hypotheses and proving them
musical	discerning sounds, their pitch, tone, rhythm, and timbre
spatial	visualizing the world in 3D
nutralist	understanding the living things and reading nature

1. **Naturalist intelligence** is the understanding of living things. A naturalist is hands on, but can recognize and categorize things easily, like animals and nature.
2. **Musical intelligence** is someone who prefers sounds and patterns. They enjoy pitch, tone and rhythm, and how this can impact emotions.
3. **Logical-Mathematical** intelligence is someone who succeeds at problem solving or performing calculations. They can make sense of patterns, categories, and relationships between different things.
4. **Existential intelligence** is the capability to question the deeper meaning, with a focus on human existence.
5. **Interpersonal intelligence** looks at the feelings and motives of others. This influences the way we act and respond appropriately to different situations and scenarios.
6. **Bodily-Kinesthetic intelligence** is a more hands-approach as they are skillful at handling objects. This is about your mind and body working in harmony together.
7. **Linguistic intelligence** is well developed verbal skills. They often consider the meanings and rhythms of words too.
8. **Intrapersonal intelligence** is when you are in tune with your values and beliefs, as well as your

feelings. This is often focused on self-awareness and they have a strong thought process.
9. **Spatial -visual intelligence** places their efforts on pictures, images, and other visual aids. It can help the learner to visualize. [11]

As well as appealing to different brain functions, mind mapping can also appeal to our different intelligences too.

The most obvious intelligence is spatial, because it is a visual aid. You are using pictures, images and colors to create your diagram, but words can also be used too. Words used in a process map are often brief, but this still appeals to the linguistic intelligence. Words can be powerful prompts. Mind maps also appeal to the kinesthetic intelligence too, because their creation means you take a hands-on approach when you produce this and it is in sync with your thoughts and ideas. As visuals encourage free, creative thinking, they also appeal to intrapersonal, existential, musical and interpersonal intelligences too. This is because the brain is prompted by images, symbols and words, which in turn can appeal to our emotions. They can encourage us to think and question, ideas and concepts further, and can stretch our thought process based on our values and beliefs. When producing a map, you need to be able to shape your thoughts in a rational way. Our human nature encourages us to make sense of things and as the naturalist is good at recognizing and categorizing, it also appeals to this intelligence too.

Visual maps are flexible. They appeal to different learning styles, different intelligences, and they activate the different parts of the brain. As a result, they are an effective learning tool, because they have a little something for everyone. Gardner also claimed that human potential is linked to our learning preferences. They are great at unlocking and utilizing learning potential, by improving our memory and thought process. [12]

Memory and Repetition

Another way of learning depends on the way our memory processes information. Visual aids can help our memory as we mentioned in the last section, but how do we remember? Words, images and symbols can all act as a prompt we have a whole learning process to go through first.

The Concise Learning Method is a proven technique used to help us to become better at studying, by improving our memory. It is a systematic approach to learning using visual and cognitive aids. Concise Learning Method makes learning easier, as there are 5 simple phases to follow. Check out the 5P process below to see how visual maps can work hand in hand with Concise Learning Method:

Phase 1: Preview - Get familiar with your topic. You need to understand key concepts and ideas. You could make a brainstorm-style mind map of what you already know about a specific topic, idea or concept, and then note down which areas you need to research further. Brainstorming is discussed in chapter 5 of this book.

Phase 2: Participate - You should always engage with the topic you are learning. Note down or ask questions and discuss ideas. Mind maps are great for notetaking too. This is covered in chapter 7.

Phase 3: Process – Review your notes and give yourself time to process the information as it needs to transfer from your short-term memory to the long-term memory. A visual map helps with this, especially if this is organized into a logical order, and uses both images and color as discussed in chapter 4.

Phase 4: Practice – Review your notes again as repetition is a great way to embed information into the memory. You can then try to solve any problems or issues that become apparent to you. Think about the concepts and ideas and consider the problems you face. It's good to take a more hands-on approach, as this will give you time to really consider the topic and reflect on your learning. Reflecting on the map and your ideas will help you memorize and process the information effectively.

Phase 5: Produce – Now it's time to critically review the information. You need to take a fresh approach, so it is often a good idea to leave your map and review this a day or two later. This is another example of how mind maps can help as they encourage free and creative thinking, so they can help you to develop new concepts, expand your thoughts, raise questions, and express further ideas.

Once you have your initial draft, it becomes easier for you to identify the key concepts and produce a mind map that concentrates on organizing and connecting your concepts, using a visual map. Repetition helps to embed information in the mind. A teacher often uses drilling techniques to help their students remember key information and this is a form of repetition. For instance, think about when we learn our times tables in school. We practice and repeat the sums and answers over and over, so that when someone asks a times table question, our brain is automatically prompted to say the answer.

Teacher: What is 8 x 5?

Student: 40.

A visual map will deepen your understanding as you consider the most relevant areas and your most unique ideas. Connecting your points and ideas will encourage you to think critically and form conclusions. Critical thinking is a cognitive approach and it can help you to examine and evaluate effectively. [13]

Listening

Listening is another great way to learn. You can note down your ideas and repeat information. Repetition is always good to drill information as listening is part of the verbal-linguistics intelligence, it is a popular way of learning. When we listen, we look at the person speaking, so this does require energy, especially as we must make sense, absorb and process the information we hear.

Making notes, using images and colors can be important to embed the information we've just heard. Remember, when listening, it is easy to become distracted, so take a breath and try to maintain your focus.

When you have finished listening, you should take some quite time to process the information. You can then review your notes. Allow your mind to organize the information in your mind and again, note down any questions as you absorb the information.

It's safe to say that visual maps and diagrams are great learning tools. They are extremely versatile and can also be used to analyze and to set goals. They can help to create a healthier mind, because the map is your planned journey to your ideal future. If you are stressed, you could make a mind map of what stresses you out. You could then add onto this, discussing three ways to address this. If you know what is stressing you out and you have a plan of how to approach this, this can really improve how you feel because it helps you to concentrate on how you can move forward. There are so many benefits of mind mapping and in the next chapter, it's time to write your own, with our step-by-step guidance.

4

How to Make a Mind Map

In this section, we will guide you through making your very own mind map. We will also explore the different components we might use when producing this, and we'll also think about how we can use them effectively. There are lots of different reasons why we might create a mind map, but typically we should be looking at expanding our current idea or concept. We also need to be familiar with the topic, or we might need to use mind maps to research this further.

Once you have your topic in mind, you will need to use a series of questions to help you expand your thoughts. Ask yourself the following questions before you create your mind map:

What is your overall goal or objective? Think about what your result will be and what you hope to achieve. For instance, if you are planning to write a book, then your goal might be to write your book within a certain amount of time. That's your result!

What is my central idea? You can form your central idea, based on your goal or objective. If writing a book is your end goal, then your central idea is your 'book'.

What do I need to know? Think about what information or knowledge you need in order to complete your mind map. Maybe you need to know things like the genre of your book, for example, and how many words or chapters you will be writing. This will give you a foundation and you will begin to understand what you are planning.

What questions do I have? Form some important questions that you need to answer when forming your mind map. Use how, what, when, where, why and who questions as this will start to expand your thoughts.

Noting and Brainstorming Ideas

We will discuss brainstorming in detail, in chapter 5. It is important to recognize the significance of brainstorming or noting down our initial thoughts, when forming a strong central idea or concept.

A brainstorm can really help you to explore your ideas while they are fresh in your brain, before they are finalized. You can note down and expand your ideas by branching off ideas from your central concept or idea.

- COOKING / BAKING
- BEAUTY PRODUCTS
- PARENTING ADVICE
- LIFESTYLE
- CRAFTS
- MAKE UP
- FILM / MUSIC / BOOKS

I want to create a blog... What should I write about?

43

For example, you might decide you want to create a blog, but you might not know what theme you want to base this on. You could start brainstorming your ideas, to narrow down your blog and this help you to form your initial idea. See below:

Once you have some topic ideas you can assess which will be the strongest. If we use the example again of blogging, you can ask yourself:

Which topic/s do I know most about?

What is my strongest topic?

Where does my knowledge lie?

You should then think of an end goal at this point.

What do you want to achieve?

Based on the example above, the end goal is to create a blog. You can then turn your thoughts into a central idea because once you know what you will be writing about, you know your end goal, you will have a theme and you can start to plan your pages, colors, themes and blog posts. This is the information you can turn into a mind map.

Create A Mind Map in Five Steps

When creating our first, basic, mind map, there are five simple steps we can follow:

Step 1 - Before you begin, you need to have paper, images (or you can draw these if you prefer), colored pens or pencils, and an idea. Alternatively, some people choose to create a mind map using computer software. There are specialist packages that you can buy, or you could use design packages like PowerPoint or Publisher.

Step 2 - First, you need to detail your central idea in the center of your diagram. This central idea is there to help you to think and expand your thoughts. Make it as colorful as you can! You could even use a diagram if you prefer. Your central idea will help you radiate your thoughts.

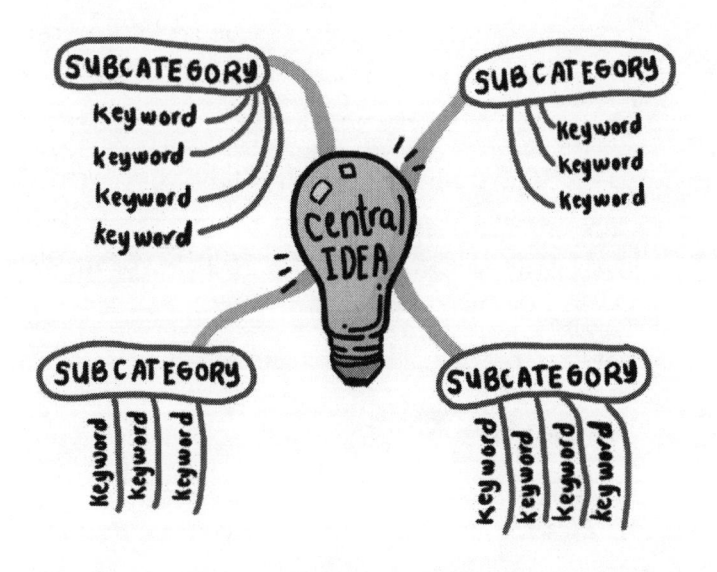

Step 3 -Add curved branches to your map that stem from the central idea. If you have started to note down ideas or brainstorm already, then you will know approximately how many subtopics will stem from your initial idea. A mind map is flexible, so you can always add further branches as you go along. Say if your central idea is to start a teaching/training business for instance, then you could map out your business model. Each branch would represent a product or service that your business offers. Say you offer four or five, you can space them out around the central idea. You may

decide later to add some further products or services, for instance, you could offer some teaching resources, and they can be added to your mind map at any time. You should color code your branches too, to help you know and understand what you are discussing. A mind map shouldn't restrict you, so any time you think of a further product or service, you should add these to your map.

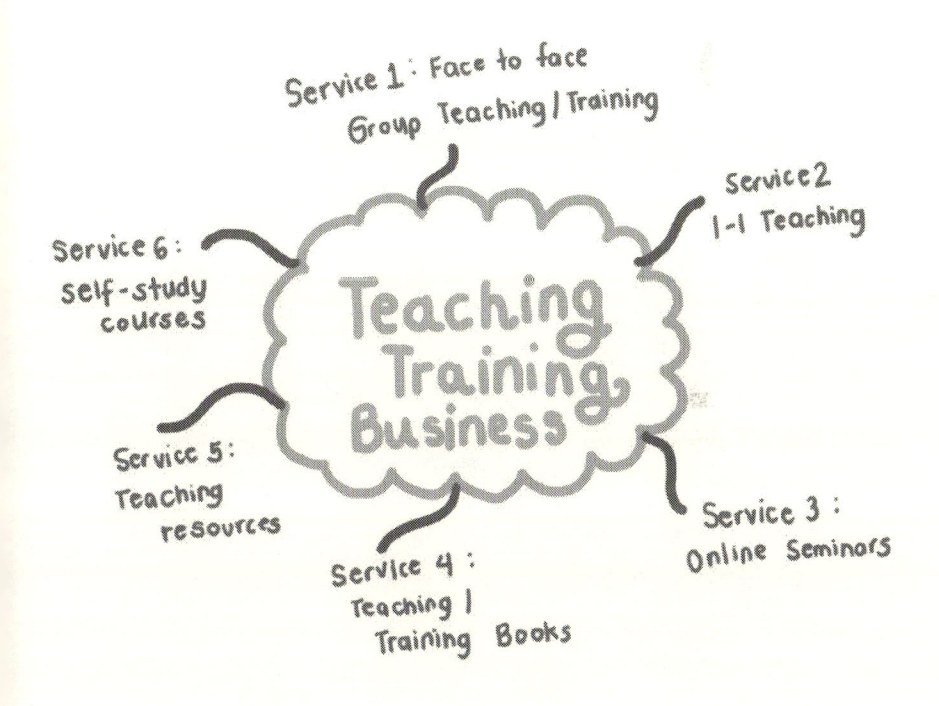

Teaching Training Business

- Service 1: Face to face Group Teaching / Training
- Service 2: 1-1 Teaching
- Service 3: Online Seminars
- Service 4: Teaching / Training Books
- Service 5: Teaching resources
- Service 6: Self-study courses

Step 4 - You should use key words or images (or both) to indicate your subtopic ideas. Now although details are important, you wouldn't go into detail during this process. You would simply list words, or images here, because a mind map is a collection of your thoughts and it can also prompt or remind you. You can explore your ideas further later, but at the time of production, it's very important just to list key words or images. Using a single word can help you to explore an idea further. For instance, if you wanted to start a business creating wedding invitations, but you simply used the word 'wedding' or 'invitations', you could have so many ideas that stem from this. For example, you could create invitations for various occasions, so limiting yourself to wedding would not be necessary. You could have christening, birthday, anniversary and event invites too. You may decide to take your business in a different direction, for example, you could focus on weddings. You could then look at including dresses, favors, venues, cakes, honeymoons, and gifts as an extra part of your business. Brainstorming this idea means you that could end up having a great idea which results in business growth.

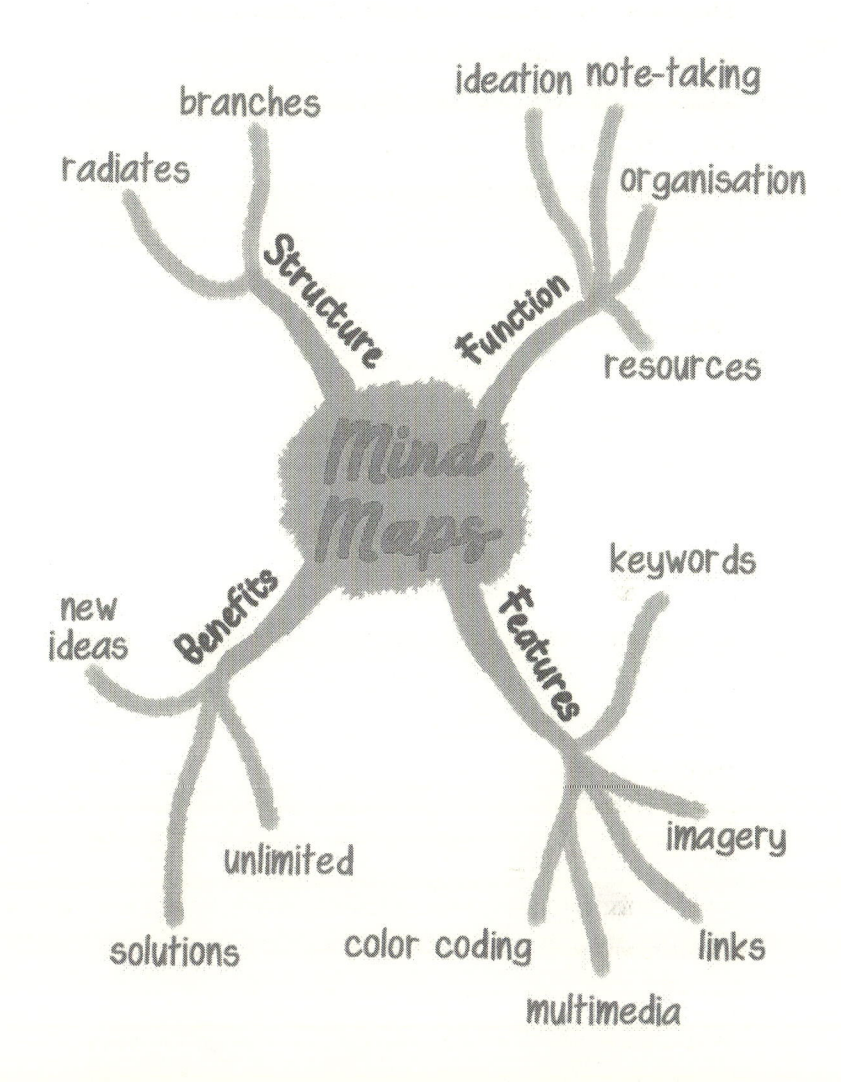

```
         branches        ideation  note-taking
  radiates                        organisation
                Structure   Function
                                   resources
                    Mind
                    Maps
                                   keywords
    new      Benefits    Features
    ideas
                                   imagery
     solutions  unlimited    color coding    links
                              multimedia
```

Step 5 - Once you've noted down your key words and/or images, you can review your mind map to see if any further ideas spring to mind. Our mind works in mysterious ways, and once we form one idea, we spark our thoughts and think of further ideas and concepts. You can use smaller branches to form further ideas from your initial subtopic ideas. Word association is useful here! If you see a word and it automatically makes you think of another, then add this to a smaller branch. Again, you can use images, colors and shapes too, as these add energy to your map. This can also encourage your imagination and creative mind!

Components of a Mind Map

A mind map mirrors the structure of the brain and because of this, it promotes creative and radiant thinking. We discussed these in the earlier chapters. It is important to build a map in a way that helps you to organize your ideas effectively and using the different components of a mind map can really aid its creation and help it make sense to you. In this section we will look at how shapes, colors, lines, images and key words/text can bring your thoughts and ideas together to create a strong, visually appealing, mind map.

Shapes – Shapes are commonly used in a mind map to represent the different parts. Usually an oval or cloud shape is used to identify the central idea or concept, and this is situated in the center of the diagram. Thick curved lines, also called branches, are used to stem from the central area of the mind map and key words are written along these to represent a subtopic or secondary idea. Thinner curved lines, often called twigs, highlight further ideas from each of the subtopic/secondary ideas. They often have key words written against them too, and they are often formed from word associations from the subtopic/secondary ideas as ideas grow. Forming these shapes helps us to organize our ideas, as everything links together. We know what the subtopics/secondary ideas stem from the central idea, and then smaller word associative ideas, flow from the subtopic/secondary idea because everything is interconnected.

Colors – Colors are also used to organize our ideas. If we have a pink branch that demonstrates our secondary ideas, then thinner twigs from this, show that the other ideas are linked to an idea or theme. Colors also enhance our learning ability. They bring vibrancy and attract our attention, thus encouraging further creative thoughts. Using colors can boost our learning and comprehension, and they also act as prompts. If we present a colorful map to others, it is more attractive, engaging and it can appear more professional too.

51

If our map and ideas are displayed in an artistic way, it can prompt us to think creatively.

Lines – Lines are an important part of the mind mapping diagram. You are encouraged to use curved lines, rather than straight lines, because they flow easier and creative thinking is not linear. The curved lines represent the way that our thoughts emit from our brain and reflect its natural pattern. The thicker branches indicate our stronger ideas that stem from the central idea or thought. The smaller twigs indicate further thoughts based on the key words from the thicker branches. The lines indicate links between ideas and help us to form word associative patterns too.

Images – Images are attractive to the eye, but they are also used to prompt our memory, because imagery helps us to remember information. We can use pictures and images that mean something to us personally. You can hand draw or hand pick your images and pictures, and they can act as a verbal cue to boost your memory and mind power. They help you to recall information, facts and ideas easily. You can use both words and images in your visual map.

Text/key words – Ideally, single words should be used when mind mapping, wherever possible. Many people think that being limited to one word is restrictive, but this can in fact empower you. You should write your key words on the branches and twigs, following their curved structure, and you can even write the word in your color of choice for that particular idea or theme. We discussed earlier in this chapter that one key word can prompt our creativity and thoughts, rather than prevent it. Allow the words to flow through your mind and free your thoughts.

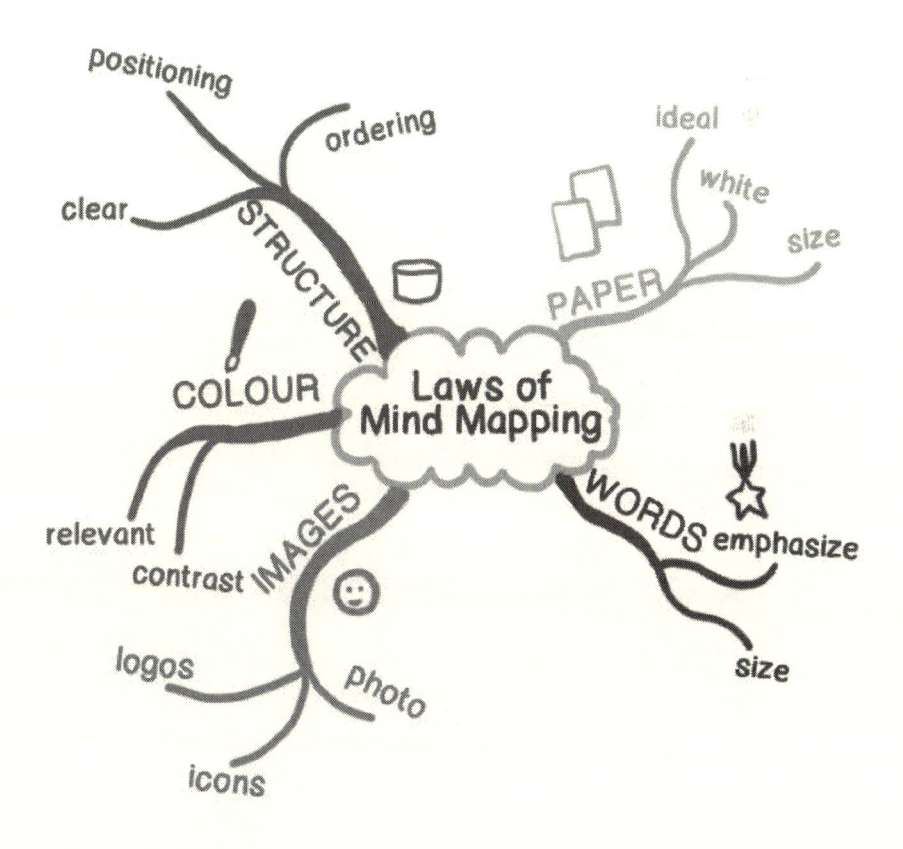

Mind map: Laws of Mind Mapping — STRUCTURE (positioning, ordering, clear), PAPER (ideal, white, size), WORDS (emphasize, size), IMAGES (relevant, contrast, logos, photo, icons), COLOUR.

53

A well-structured mind map, uses strong key words, and is visually appealing with colors and images can really aid the thought process. It can generate ideas and help you build a bigger picture so that you can coordinate any complex project with ease. Your mind map uses your thoughts and brain power to paint a picture in your mind and this can increase the way you retain information. We become clear in what we must do to achieve our end goal and that once complex project, is planned so well, it makes sense and seems much simpler.

A well-planned visual map can make us feel much more confident in ourselves and our abilities, because we know how will move forward.

Now we have an idea of how you can create a simple mind map, you should try this out.

Once you can create a general mind map, the whole process will become easier and you can start working on bespoke versions, tailored to your specific style, topic and needs.

5

Brainstorming with Mind Maps

Brainstorming is a common way to generate your thoughts and ideas. They are the first stage of initiating ideas, so this is often a kind of notetaking exercise that helps you think consider new ideas, that you may not have looked at previously. You are not limited to single words with a brainstorm, as you can list questions, and use phrases, as well as pictures.

Brainstorms can be completed by an individual, but they are more common as a form of group work. With brainstorming, everyone's ideas and opinions can be shared without any inhibitions or expectations – no idea is devalued.

A brainstorm is a quick, easy way to get down your idea. It's often less appealing, visually, than a focused mind map with a clear central idea. There are some benefits of brainstorming techniques as they are flexible, and you can include more detail if you wish, as you are not limited to just one word. They are less appealing visually, people usually use words and phrases, they often don't use color or images. The idea of the 'brainstorm' is to eject ideas from a person/s brain, straight onto the page, without thinking too much about it. They can be a little messy, but they represent how your brain flicks through different ideas. You can return to them later and make them pretty as you start to make sense of your thoughts and ideas.

Brainstorms are a basic form of mind maps and in order to do this effectively, you need a topic or central idea. Brainstorming can also be used to thrash out problems and possible solutions, so you can use this as your central idea. Although this is a straightforward, free-thinking tool, there are some simple guidelines to consider before we begin.

The Rules of Brainstorming

Brainstorming is meant to be creative, and the environment should be comfortable. Some ideas will be used and expanded further, while others will not. That doesn't mean that any idea is incorrect as the most important thing is acceptance: acceptance of other ideas, and acceptance that our ideas may not be used further. Everyone should be made aware of the guidelines below:

1. No idea is judged by anyone.
2. The wilder the idea, the better.
3. Quantity over quality – don't think too much!
4. Every person is valued, and their ideas are as equally worthy.
5. You should consider all ideas and expand on these. Remember that if you work as a group, you should all take ownership for every idea and expand on that.

As brainstorming is an idea generating tool, we can use the format of the brainstorm to stretch our thoughts. Everyone is encouraged to participate in this thought-provoking exercise. One person's idea often sparks a new idea from another person.

But what happens if we don't know what we are brainstorming? If we do not have an idea or concept in mind?

How to Come Up with Ideas (Even If You Don't Have Any)

If you don't already have an idea, you can use brainstorms to generate these because they encourage your creative thought process.

In chapter 4, we talked about having an overall goal or objective that indicated our expectations or what we wanted to achieve.

A brainstorm can simply be used as a tool to form ideas, then we might choose to break down one of those ideas into more depth, later.

Brainstorming can be as easy as A, B, C, if you follow the 3 simple steps below to generate your ideas.

A Think about your end goal and what you want to achieve, or alternatively, if you have a problem you want to solve, think about what the problem is. Write this down in the center of your diagram and make it as colorful as possible.

B Use questioning techniques to generate ideas from this central goal. Formulate prompting questions using 7 types of questions: who, what, when, where, why, how and which. Note down any ideas that spring to mind and if you're working in a group, get the others to shout out their ideas while one person notes these down, by drawing branches stemming from the center. Everyone should be able to think freely and contribute and if you are working in a group, you can use the ideas of others to generate further ideas.

C Once you have a range of ideas on the page, start to discuss and analyze these. Choose 2 or 3 ideas or solutions from the list and focus on these by analyzing further. Address each point in turn, and form a separate, simple mind map. Consider how they can help you to solve your problem or reach your end goal. You can use the guidelines in chapter 4, to transform your brainstorm, into a creative and colorful mind map, using key words and images only, based on your initial brainstorm. You can start to omit the ideas that won't work and stick to the ideas that you want to move forward with. Remember that visual maps are always a working progress, so they can be added to and amended as necessary.

How to Brainstorm When you Don't Have an End Goal

Brainstorming can work in a similar way, even if you are not sure of what your end goal or problem is. In truth, you must have some idea of what you are brainstorming, even if it is vague, otherwise how would you know that a brainstorm is needed?

Obviously, you know why you are brainstorming as you have a topic already, but you may need to discuss this further or complete research. For instance, if a business is losing money but they are not sure how, a brainstorm could be completed to highlight the different products and services offered within the business, as well as some benefits and drawbacks of each area.

Your topic in this case, is to find out why the business is losing money and to change that. A brainstorm could help you highlight the problem or make your end goal clearer, and only then, once they are clear, should you brainstorm resolutions or further ideas.

Sometimes, you may need to complete some research by asking the different people in the organization why the business is losing money, what problems they face, or what they think is the biggest challenge faced by the business. You can use the 7 questions detailed in B, of the A, B, C process in the earlier section, to research your topic. From this, you can formulate your end goal or highlight your problem. The important thing is not to rush into creating your brainstorm. Don't be afraid to make a rough draft first and investigate until you are satisfied. Even if you are detailing a problem, you will still have an end goal, as you will still know what you hope to achieve by the end of your brainstorming session.

CASE STUDY

Judy is a team leader in a call centre, and she needs to improve customer satisfaction scores within her team. The team's customer satisfaction is 7.9% on average, and her manager has told her that they should improve to 8.5%. Judy has three months to make these improvements, but she has to feed back to her manager in two weeks to inform him of how the team plan to improve. Good customer service is instrumental in gaining further customer contracts, so this is something that Judy must prioritize.

Here are some examples of the questions Judy might want to consider before carrying out a brainstorming session:

What do I need to do? In order to improve customer satisfaction, Judy needs to find out exactly what the problem is. She researches the customer satisfaction figures for her team to see if anything stands out or indicates the issues. She finds that the team scored low on customer waiting times, when calling the team. She looks for a correlation between the results and finds that customer waiting times are longer during the hours 10 – 11 AM and 12 – 2 PM.

How should I implement this improvement? She decides to facilitate a brainstorming session with her team to address this improvement and discuss a way forward. She plans to present the results to the team, so that they can work together on a solution.

Who is involved in this session? All team members will attend this brainstorming session.

Where is the improvement needed? Customer telephone waiting times during the hours of 10 – 11 AM and 12 – 2 PM.

When is the improvement needed? The team have two weeks to put a plan of action in place.

Why? The company have stressed that it is very important for the team to improve. In a performance-based business, customers are at the heart and if a team isn't performing, jobs can be at risk. It is important that the team act. That is why a brainstorming session is ideal for Judy and her team, because they can all take ownership of the results and work together to improve.

What is her goal? The goal of Judy's team is to improve customer satisfaction from 7.9% to 8.5% within the next three months and has two weeks to put a plan of action in place. This means she must figure out what is causing the problem in the first place.

Judy is now ready for her group brainstorming session with her team.

Take another look at Judy's goal in the case study above. Her goal is SMART!

What is a SMART Goal?

Once you have started to formulate an end goal idea, ensure it is SMART:

Specific – Ensure your goal is as specific as possible and spells out what you want to achieve.

Measurable – Your end goal must be measurable, so that progress can be measured. A measure is something concrete, that can be counted. For example, if you want to gain 10 new customers within a 3-month period, and you assess your progress after month 1, and find that you already have 5 new customers you will know that you are well on way to meeting/achieving your end goal.

Achievable – Your end goal should be achievable, because if a goal is not achievable, you are setting yourself up to fail. Ensure your goals are possible. For example, say you want to sell a product to 100 people within a week, but you do not have time or means to implement an effective marketing strategy, then it is likely that this will not be possible, and therefore is not achievable.

Realistic – As an end goal needs to be achievable, it needs to be realistic in the same way. Be real about what you can achieve and what is realistic based on your own circumstances. Ask yourself is this possible?

Timely – A goal should always have a timescale or limit attached to it. This is also a good measuring tool. If I simply said I wanted to gain 100 customers, it might take me 5 years to achieve this as this goal is not clear. Time and effort may not be spent on this specific goal, as it does not have a timescale and therefore its urgency is unclear. Timescales give us something to work towards and a deadline to work to.

Once you have a draft copy and a clear end goal, you can go back to the previous section and begin brainstorming your ideas, based on that end goal once more.

A brainstorm-style mind map is ideal to begin generating your ideas, but sometimes we need a more tailored visual map. For example, we might choose them to plan writing, for notetaking and even when planning a business model. We can use mind mapping techniques for personal reasons too, like planning your wedding!

We will now explore the diverse mind mapping techniques available to us.

6

Mind Mapping for Writing

Mind mapping is a great way to plan your writing, from creative writing, to essay writing, and even copywriting. We can use them to extend our thought process and it's possible to develop and improve our writing too. This chapter is for you if you want to use visual maps for writing!

How to Write Better

It is a known fact that we tend to write better if we plan our writing. That's not to say that we should avoid free writing and hold back our creativity, as planning should inspire and prompt us to explore our ideas further. Mind maps are often used by teachers and often, they will show this technique to their students, to help improve their writing or learning experience.

Writing is something that we do daily. I don't necessarily mean writing in the literal sense, so let's imagine that by writing we mean putting words onto a page, whether this is handwritten or in an electronic format. In fact, it's hard to imagine a day without writing. We write to-do lists in the coffee shop, put together an email at work, or make notes in our notebook while we're on public transport. If we send a text message or use an app that dictates our words for us, we are still putting those words on the page and therefore, we are essentially writing.

In order to create your mind map, you will need:

- ✓ A piece of paper (A4 or A5)
- ✓ A pencil
- ✓ An eraser
- ✓ A ruler (optional)
- ✓ A pen
- ✓ Colored pens, markers, pencils, etc.

Mind maps can help us to write better. Whether you are planning an essay, a book, fiction or non-fiction, mind maps can work, and they can help us to be clear and effective when writing.

But how?

How to Write an Essay

If you want to use mind maps when planning an essay there are two ways to approach this. If you don't already have a research question or topic in mind, then you may wish to start off by brainstorming your initial ideas. This is discussed in chapter 5 and this method will be ideal if you don't have a clear direction. Once you've brainstormed your topic or research question, you can return to this section and plan your essay writing.

See the image below for an example of a visual map that lists the research question, any topics you wish to explore and any ongoing themes and theories that can be explored further:

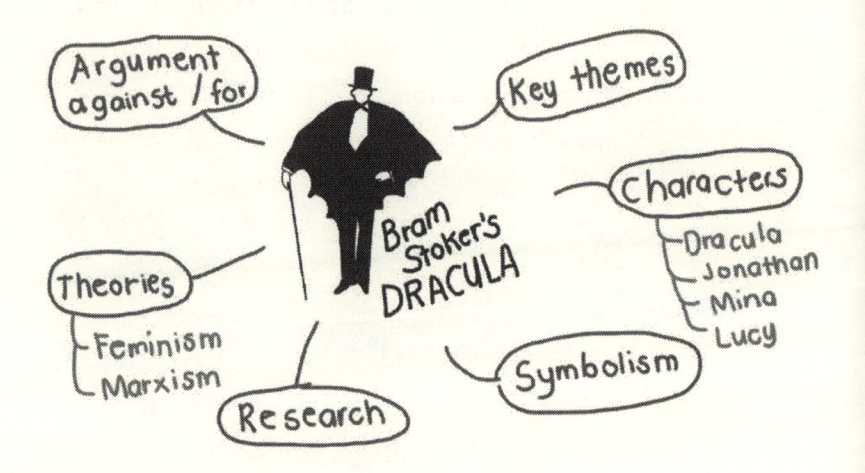

Mind map diagram: central node "Bram Stoker's DRACULA" with branches to:
- *Argument against / for*
- *Key themes*
- *Characters* — Dracula, Jonathan, Mina, Lucy
- *Symbolism*
- *Research*
- *Theories* — Feminism, Marxism

We will look at using mind maps when taking notes and studying in more detail, in the next chapter!

If you already have a research question or topic in mind, then we can use this central idea to generate a plan for a concise, well-written, and well-researched essay. Start off with a central idea in the middle of your paper. This could be your topic of interest or your research question. Draw a border around this, like a cloud or oval shape.

You should then branch off from this into four key sections:

1. **Research** – Branch off into subcategories like, books, journals, any experiments or studies

you've conducted yourself, online resources, for instance, and then you can use twigs, to form a list of your different research materials and methods. Remember to add links or page numbers were necessary as they will be useful for referencing and citation purposes.

2. **Structure** – Consider the word count, the construction of your essay (introduction, literary review, comparisons/discussions/arguments throughout the body of the essay, conclusion, recommendations, bibliography) and also, how you will structure your time.

3. **Argument in support of your research question/topic** – You can complete this part of your map when you are beginning your initial research. Note down key arguments you decide to use in your essay, in support of your argument.

4. **Argument in opposition of your research question/topic** – Again, you might not know this until you start to research but note down key arguments you decide to use that opposes your supporting argument. Use your counter argument to indicate what you agree or disagree with, based on the evidence.

Here are five important tips when completing your essay writing mind map:

- Make sure you are clear of your overall goal or research question.
- Don't research everything. Only select the relevant areas of the research for your essay, that addresses your research question. For example, don't read the whole book, if only chapter 3 covers your research area.
- Use colored pens to signify each subtopic/idea, along with related ideas that stem from that.
- Look at your structure and note down an approximate word count for each section.
- When you list your arguments in support, write an opposing argument against this, in the opposing section. Always review the benefits and drawbacks.

How To Create an Essay Plan

When you have your completed mind map in front of you, you can start to form an essay plan. Begin with the structure and think about what you want to include in each section. You should cross reference the sources you are going to use to set the scene with your methodology, and clearly state what you are arguing. Your argument is the stance that you are taking here, it's your interpretation. When planning the body of your essay remember to note which arguments/sources for or opposing that you plan to include. Your conclusion should be built on the strength of your arguments and sources. You should clearly state what you have discovered or proved as a result of your research.

How to Plan-out a Book for Authors

One of the most difficult parts of writing a book is keeping track of your goals and ideas. Mind maps can be a great way to help you form a plan and play out the whole process, as well as planning out the content of your book.

We will start at the beginning by thinking about the book process and this will ensure that you do everything you need to do at the right time, during the writing process.

First of all, you should write your central idea in the center of your paper. This could be the title of your book (if you know this) or you might write down a goal or a question like:

How will I write my book, publish my book and market my book, effectively? , or

Write, publish and write a book by (date).

Once you have this detailed you can start to link off to your subtopic areas. Use different colors to represent each section.

✓ You may want to choose a topic for your book and think about any possible subgenres too.

✓ In another section, you may want to think about your audience and what they want. Who is your ideal reader?

✓ Think about your competition and place yourself in the market. What books are similar to yours? How is your book different (nobody wants to read something that's exactly the same as something else)? What books are selling right now?

✓Publication options should be considered. Will your book be available in hard copy or as an eBook (both is possible too)? Will you be pitching to an agent? Will you submit your writing to publishers? Which publishers specialize in your chosen genre? Think about the timescale of this process. Is self-publishing an option?

✓ You should think about any profits you expect to make from your publication. The market is constantly changing and how much you will make can really depend on the publication method you choose. When considering your profits, you should also consider any costs incurred from writing the book. Maybe you hired an Editor or paid for advertising. Those costs need to be met, before you count your profit.

✓ Write down a draft contents page or chapter list. You may wish to create a chapter outline, separate to your mind map. Assign timescales to your chapters, as this will help you to plan the time you'll spend on your book.

✓ How will people recognize you as an author? Make yourself known as an author. Start by sharing information with your friends and family. You should also use social media to increase your visibility. Post snippets from your book and get people excited about its launch. Hook them in!

✓ Another subsection to include is the marketing your book. List ideas in this section that indicate how you plan to launch and market your book. You should also include any networking opportunities, for instance if you are attending any events or plan to do a reading in a bookstore or a library. You could ask other people or magazines to interview you.

✓ Make future plans – what do you want from this book? Think about releasing five copies of your book a week early for free, in return for honest reviews. Will you write a sequel, or do you have any other books in the pipeline? [14]

Check out the image on the next page for some ideas, but don't be afraid to stray from this. Remember that mind maps are there to help encourage you to think and explore your ideas freely and creatively.

How to Plan out a Book

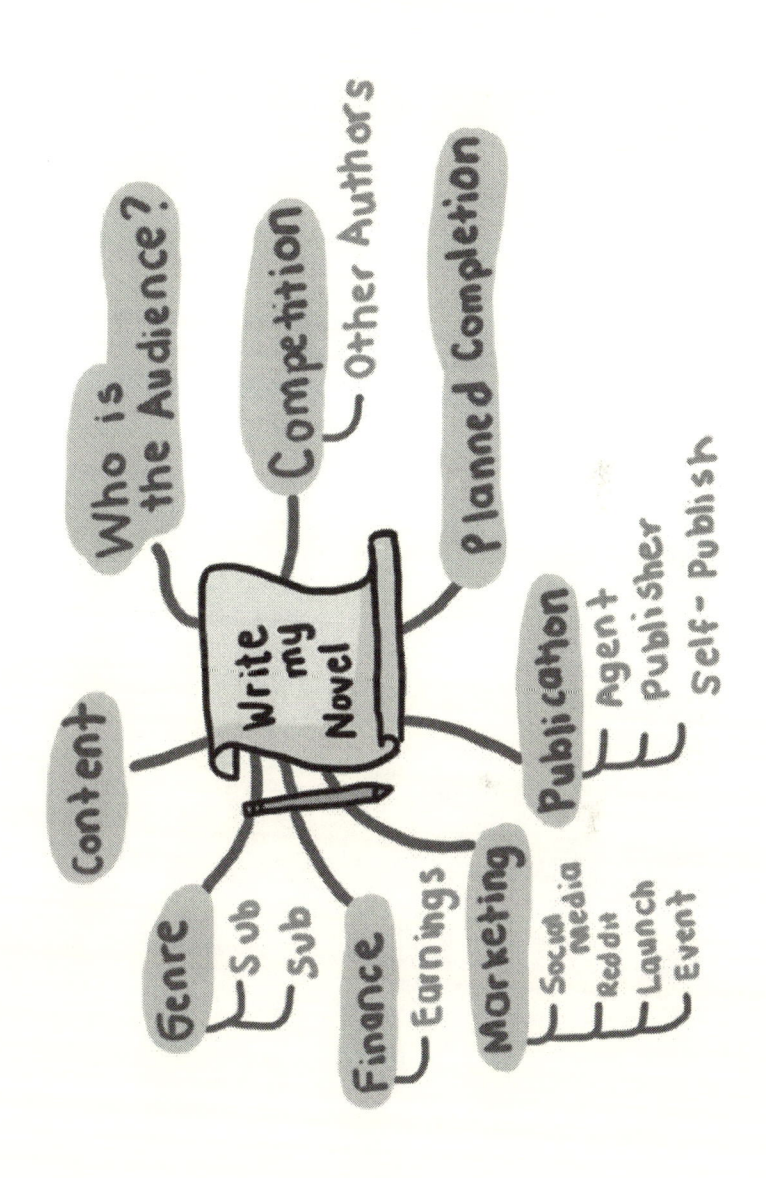

- Write my Novel
  - Who is the Audience?
  - Competition
    - Other Authors
  - Planned Completion
  - Publication
    - Agent
    - Publisher
    - Self-Publish
  - Marketing
    - Social Media
    - Reddit
    - Launch Event
  - Finance
    - Earnings
  - Genre
    - Sub
    - Sub
  - Content

Non-fiction Book Planning

If you want to plan the content of your non-fiction book, then a mind map can be useful. If you are at this stage, then you will already know the process that you are going to follow in order to produce your book, and you will already have a topic in mind. You will also be aware of the direction of your book.

For this type of visual map, you should place your central idea in the center of your paper, which is usually your book topic or title. Non-fiction books are often based around a specific idea, so you usually you wouldn't need to brainstorm things like characters, genre or setting. It is recommended that you focus on the different chapters and essential topics of interests that will make up the book, as they will be your subtopic ideas. This still leaves a broad category to explore based on your subtopic ideas.

Imagine you are writing a short non-fiction book on Small Business Accountancy. Think about subtopics that you might need to cover – for example, what constitutes as a small business? Setting financial goals, essential business records, planning a realistic financial budget, creating a five-year plan. See the diagram below to show how we can plan this type of book.

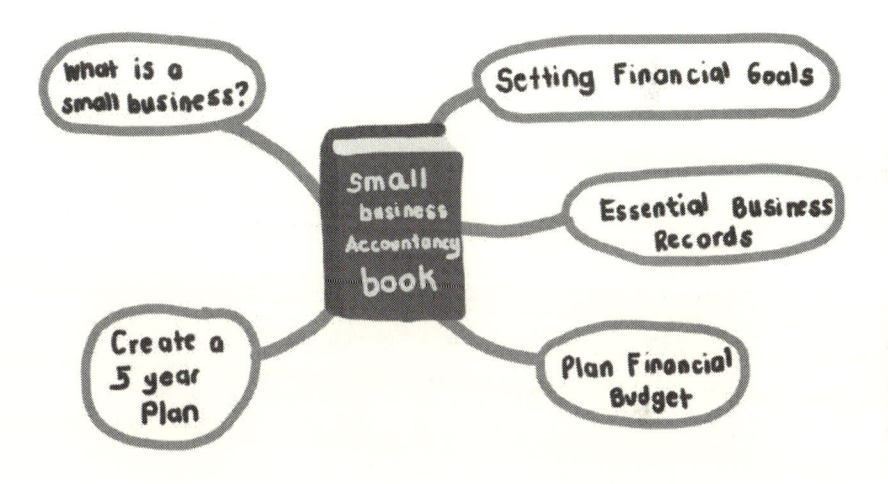

- Small business Accountancy book
  - What is a small business?
  - Setting Financial Goals
  - Essential Business Records
  - Plan Financial Budget
  - Create a 5 year Plan

Think about how you can apply this idea to your own non-fiction book idea. Think about your subtopic ideas and further ideas that radiate from that.

Fiction Book Planning

When it comes to planning your fiction book, we can approach this a little differently and yet, the concept stays the same. The good thing about planning your fiction book, is that there's more flexibility when it comes to creativity. Mind mapping can be extremely beneficial in this case.

Put your book topic or title in the center as this is your central idea. You should then focus on the following subtopic areas:

Characters – list your characters and indicate and characters that have a significant role. Think about your protagonist, the antagonist, and write one word that describes who the character is, for example, Jerry (protagonist), Anna (Jerry's love interest), Lizzie (Jerry's mother and antagonist). Remember when creating a mind map, you want to give as little detail as possible.

Setting – here you can list information about your setting. Where is your story set? Do you visit anywhere else? What's the setting like (quiet, busy, city, suburban)?

Plot – you then need to branch off further and discuss the beginning, middle and end, with further twigs that indicate ideas for each part of the plot.

Themes – list any key or recurring themes that you are including in your fictional story. The clearer you are about what you are trying to achieve, the easier it is to write.

Genre – list your key genre along with any subgenres. You can then explore further from this and list the traits/plotlines/character/setting that relates to that specific genre or subgenre.

Chapters and wordcount – list your chapters and your expected wordcount for each chapter. You can use this to draft your chapter outline, which will help you plan the direction of each chapter in your book if you haven't already.

Follow the example of the fiction mind map shown on the next page.

How to Write a Fiction Book

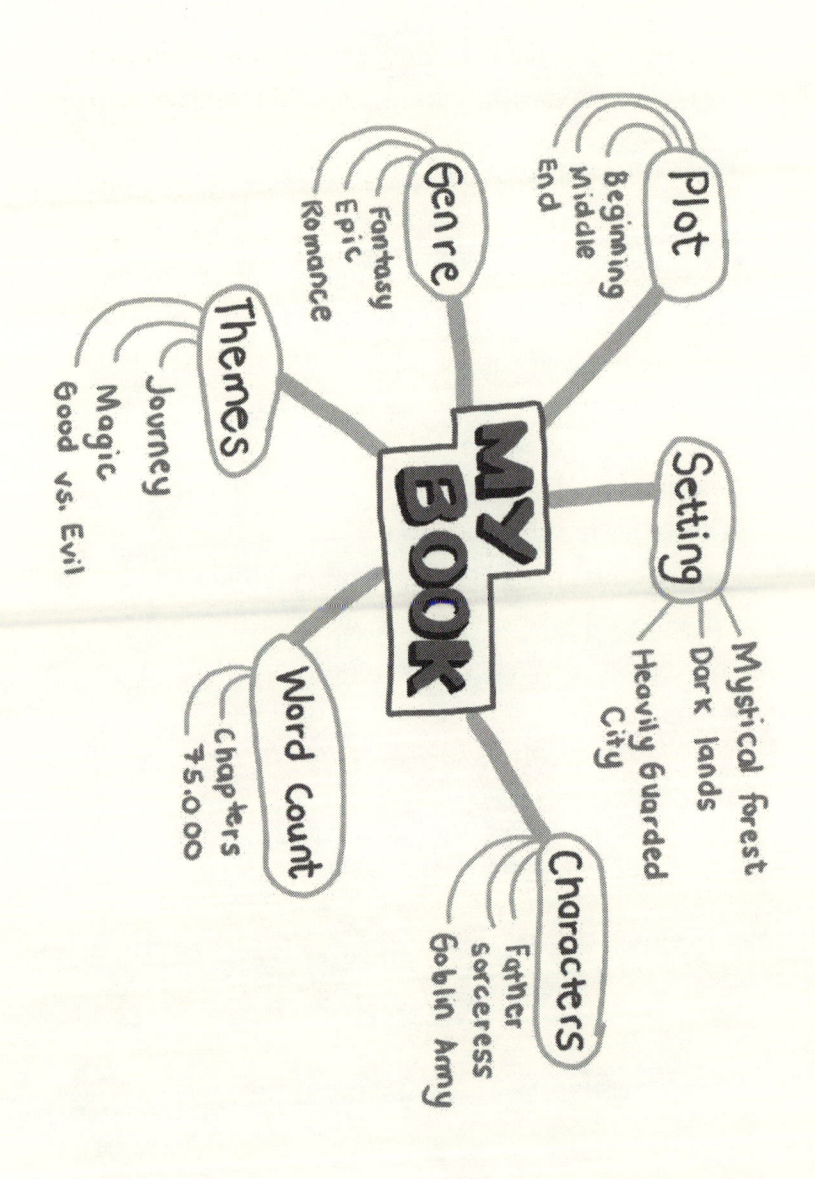

MY BOOK

- **Plot**
  - Beginning
  - Middle
  - End
- **Genre**
  - Fantasy
  - Epic
  - Romance
- **Themes**
  - Journey
  - Magic
  - Good vs. Evil
- **Word Count**
  - Chapters
  - 75,000
- **Characters**
  - Father
  - Sorceress
  - Goblin Army
- **Setting**
  - Mystical Forest
  - Dark Lands
  - Heavily Guarded City

Think about how you could tailor this diagram so that it represents your book idea.

Planning the content or process of your writing will save you a lot of time. Whether you are writing an essay, fiction or non-fiction, a visual map can help you to explore your ideas as well as helping you plan content and the writing process. This gives you clarity, helps you to pace your work and stay on topic but don't be afraid to use your creativity.

7

Notetaking with Mind Maps

Mind maps are great if you need to take notes and they also make an excellent study tool. Because mind maps are so flexible, you can incorporate and adjust them to suit your learning styles and preferences as they aid many different study styles. They often help us learn at a faster rate and make it easier for us to learn new concepts.

Notetaking, Reading and Studying with Mind Maps

Mind mapping is a great tool to use when you are notetaking. Sometimes we take notes because people are telling us something, or we are reading something that we need to know. Mind maps are great when reading, notetaking and studying as it means that you can put all of your ideas together by making a visual representation, and this can often help you to make sense of it. Reading, notetaking and studying work hand in hand, because when you are studying, you are usually reading or listening. We've already discussed creating visuals when researching in chapter 6, because creating and referring to a diagram can be an effective learning experience.

As a general style for notetaking, you may want to look at the image on the next page for a rough guide of how to set out your mind map, when preparing to take notes.

Don't forget that you can adapt this to suit your own style!

How to Write Notes

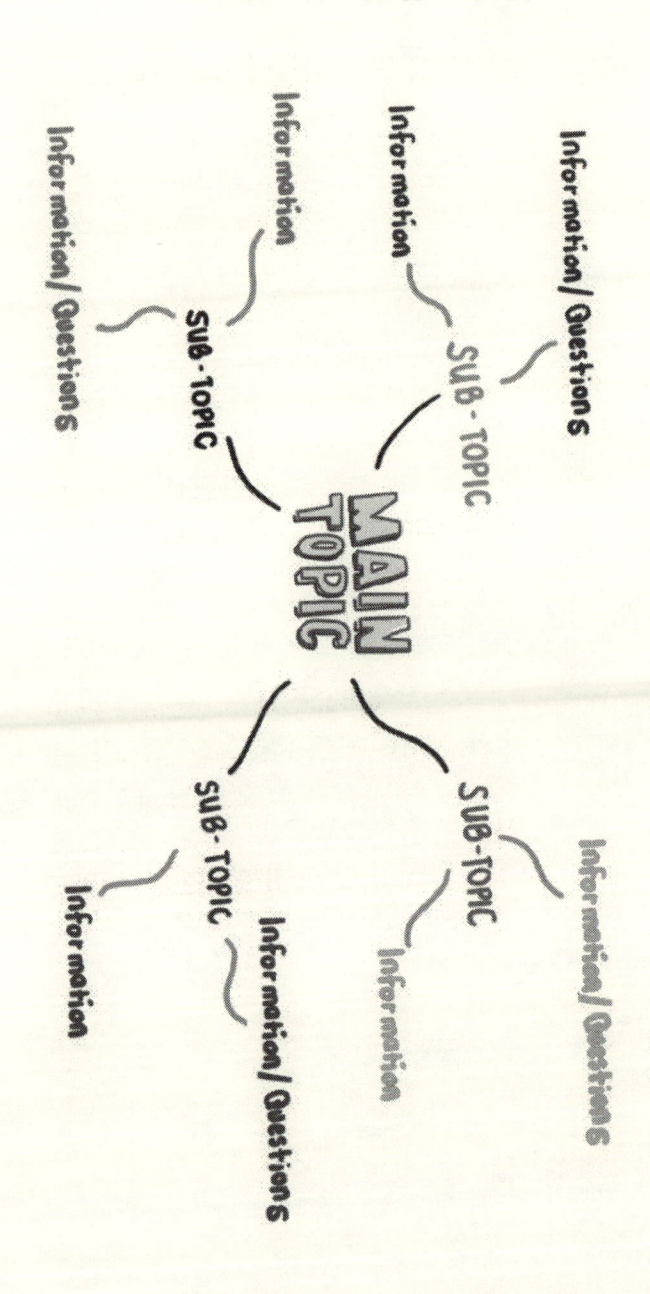

How to Take Notes of Books

If you need to analyze or study a book, mind maps are a great. You should put the book title in the center, and if you know what you are looking for, then you can create initial subtopics before you begin. For example, if you are studying fiction, then you might be looking for important themes, tropes, genres and subgenres, literary devices, symbolism, plot, and conflict. You can then branch off into other smaller ideas from each of these. As you go through the book, you might find further subtopic areas.

This diagram explores characters and their relationships in Bram Stoker's *Dracula*. This is a great example of how you might want to set out a visual map in preparation for your notetaking session, but again, don't' be afraid to adapt your map to your own style, as necessary.

Mind map: Characters + Relationships — Dracula

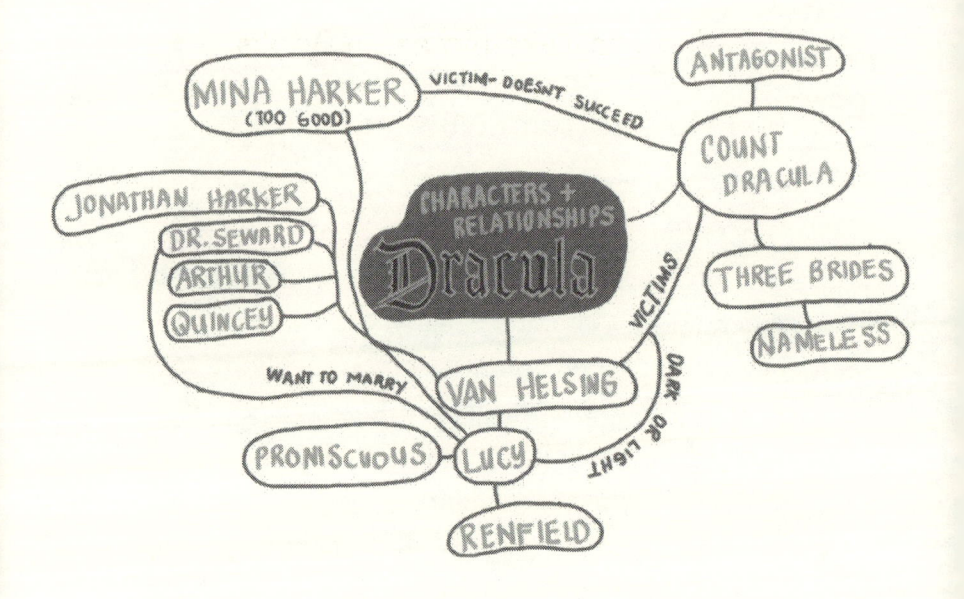

- Mina Harker (too good) — victim, doesn't succeed
- Jonathan Harker, Dr. Seward, Arthur, Quincey — want to marry Lucy
- Count Dracula — antagonist
- Three Brides, Nameless
- Van Helsing
- Lucy — promiscuous, dark or light
- Renfield
- Victims

If you are reading a non-fiction or academic book, then you might approach this differently. You may note down key quotes, lessons learned, key themes or ideas to explore. Sometimes non-fiction books recommend other sources too, so recommendations could also be a great subtopic idea in some cases.

If you need to make a summary of the book, you could either write your idea in the center with the book title, or you could construct a bibliography from mind map, and then write a short paragraph about the book's key points or topic.

How to Take Notes on Books

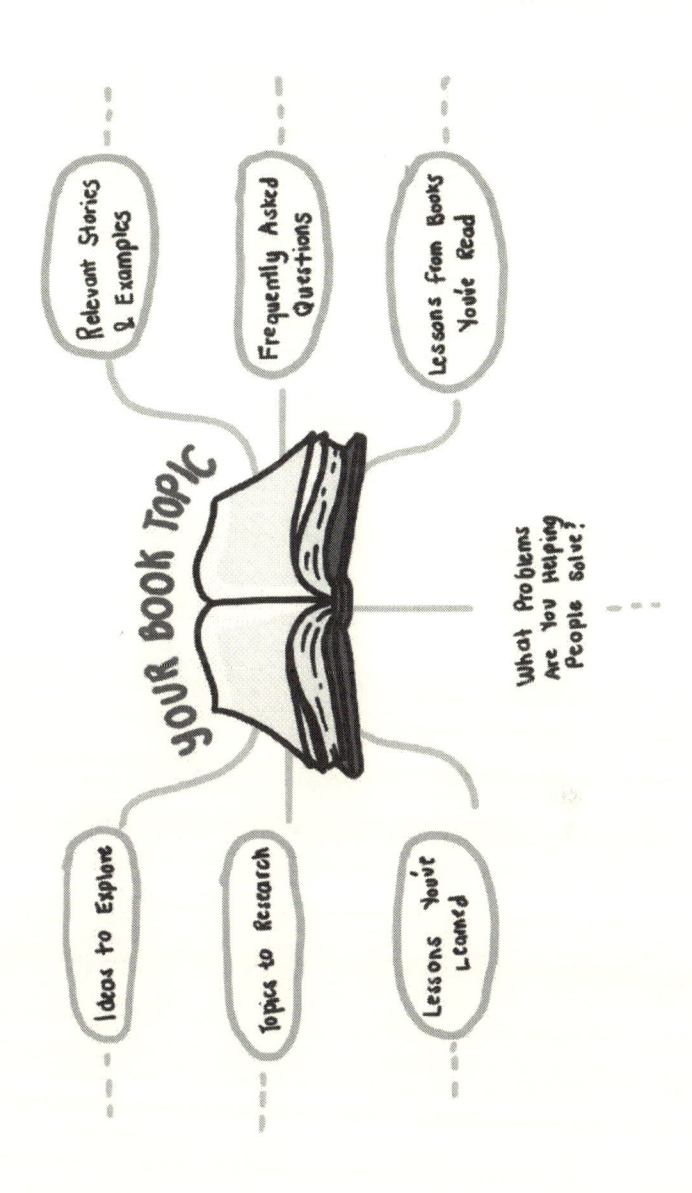

- Relevant Stories & Examples
- Frequently Asked Questions
- Lessons From Books You've Read
- Your Book Topic
- What Problems Are You Helping People Solve?
- Ideas to Explore
- Topics to Research
- Lessons You've Learned

When taking notes for books, it's important to stay focused and write as little information to prompt you, as possible. Even though you are writing down thoughts, ideas and concepts that you are taking from a book, it's still important to have your own ideas. If you have an important thought, point or question, then add that to your initial mind map to prompt your thoughts further.

How to Take Notes of Speeches or Lectures

We've just discussed how we can take notes from books, but we also often take notes when someone is talking to us or a group or people. If we need to remember something or if we are learning something, then we need effective notes that we can read back and process the information through our brain. Similar concepts can be used if you take notes at meetings, or in learning classes/workshops too!

There are 5 steps you should follow when taking notes from speeches or lectures:

1. Write the title of the lecture or speech topic as the central idea.

2. Read over the agenda or any paperwork you've received and think about anything that you might want to focus on.
3. Write as little as possible – just one or two words if possible.
4. Every time the speaker moves onto a new idea, use a branch to create a subtopic idea, and then use smaller twigs when stretching your idea further. Use colors and shapes.
5. Save a section for questions – again keep them as brief as possible, just enough information to prompt you.

Check the diagrams of the agenda and accompanying mind map template below and think about how we can follow the steps above, based on this example:

Physics : PH205
Lecture 1: Vectors

<u>Agenda</u>
What is a vector?
How to express a vector
Addition of vectors
Vectors in component form

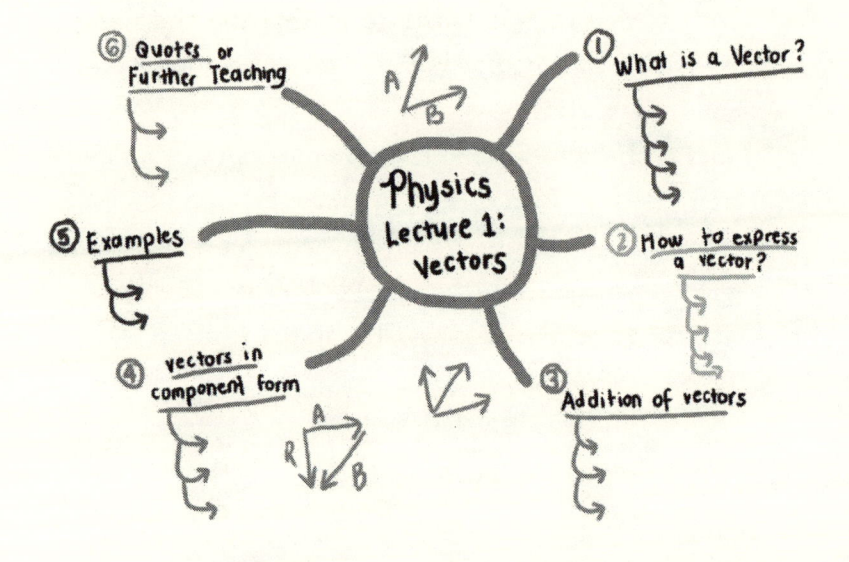

How to Create a List

We can use mind mapping concepts to create a list. Some people can find lists limiting, as usually you are just writing one-word responses or sometimes facts. They are great as they are concise, and just like a mind map, they are easily organized. Lists can be actionable for example; many people write to-do lists, and then we know each item is actionable. Lists can also be written for things we need, like a shopping list for instance.

If you want to create a list that is more complex, a mind map can help you to organize that list into subcategories. Look at the way that the shopping list below is organized:

SHOPPING LIST

- **SUNDRIES**: BIN BAGS, PEGS, LIGHTBULB
- **VEGETABLES**: POTATOES, COURGETTES, BROCCOLI, MANGE TOUT
- **STAPLES**: EGGS, BUTTER, MILK, BREAD
- **MEALS**: PASTA, SAUSAGES, STEAK, SALMON
- **DRINKS**: WATER, BEER, FRUIT JUICE, WINE, COKE
- **FRUIT**: APPLES, PEARS, BANANAS, LEMON

Think about the different things you might write a list for and imagine them in the format of a mind map...

93

8

Mind Mapping for Planning

A visual map is in fact a planning tool. It's ideal because it can really spark our imagination and promote motivation. You might be able to look at things in a different light, and start seeing changes and challenges differently. In this chapter we're going to talk about mind mapping to set goals, to embrace change, to manage your own time, to be organized, as well as to create a budget.

How to Set Goals

Using mind maps to goal set, is one of the simplest forms of mind maps, because it is focused around what we want or need (or what a business wants or needs but will refer to business later in chapter 14).

Start out by writing your central idea in the center of your paper. You can write something such as "Goals for 2020", or "My Fitness Goals" to help get you started.

You should then use branches to identify your goals. Remember that goals and objectives should be S.M.A.R.T, we discussed this in chapter 5. Your goals will act as your subtopic area.

Following this, you should have twigs coming from your subtopic area, that identify your objectives. Your objectives are the steps that you will take to achieve those goals. Give yourself time beforehand to think about what you must do in order to achieve your goal, but when you are creating your map, allow yourself to think freely – no judgement. Just because you note down some goal or objective ideas, doesn't mean that you *must* use this in this future. Often, a wild idea or thought will spark some other ideas and thoughts for future innovation.

How to Set a Goal

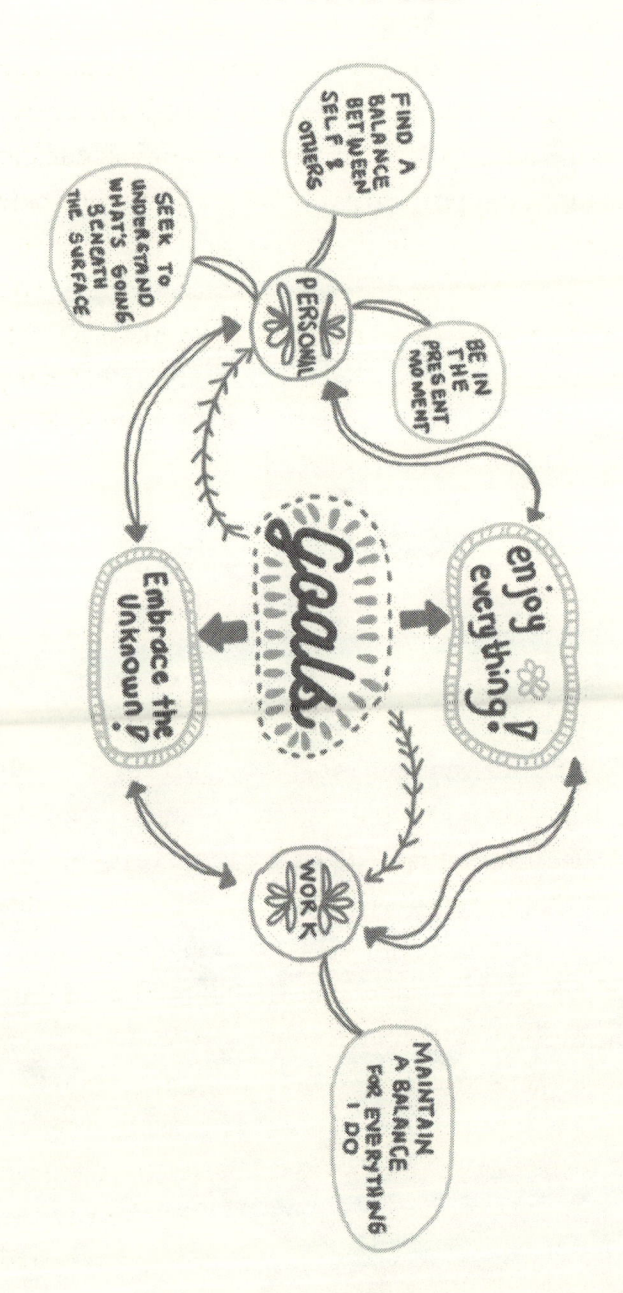

Goals

- PERSONAL
  - FIND A BALANCE BETWEEN SELF & OTHERS
  - SEEK TO UNDERSTAND WHAT'S GOING ON BENEATH THE SURFACE
  - BE IN THE PRESENT MOMENT
- Embrace the Unknown!
- enjoy everything!
- WORK
  - MAINTAIN A BALANCE FOR EVERYTHING I DO

What if I don't have any goals?

We all have dreams and if you have a dream, you have a goal; even if you can't think of it right now. You do have to take ownership when it comes to personal and business goals as only you can decide what they are. If you don't have any goals, but you know that change or development is needed, you can work back over. Ask yourself some thought-provoking questions – what do I want? What is my ideal? Where do I see myself in the future? How can I improve? Why do I want…?

How to Embrace Change

We have mentioned many times that visual maps are creative tools that encourage us to think freely, but mind maps are so much more. They can help us to problem solve and as they are also visual, it's safe to say that they are a great motivational tool.

It's inevitable that things *change* in our lives. Sometimes we choose the change whereas other times, we can feel as if change is pushed upon us. Businesses and workplaces often need to change in line with their client needs and often the law can influence change too. Businesses are then required to change, so their staff must change, and this can sometimes have a negative impact.

Change doesn't have to be negative. Change is only necessary because we have to do something different. The more we change, the more we improve our skills and develop ourselves as a person. If we feel pushed into changes, then it can be our nature to rebel against it because change can be scary. It means that something we are used to doing and currently do well, is taken away from us. This can cause doubts. *What if we fail?*

The point I'm making here, is that change is usually a good thing. We never change to make things worse or harder for ourselves, we change to make things better. Sometimes, this doesn't happen right away as we can suffer teething problems. We might have to tweak the new product, service or working method until it meets our needs – this is okay!

Let's move back to the topic of mind maps.

Look at the following case study to see how they can help us to embrace change:

CASE STUDY

Ben works for a large IT company as a Sales Consultant. The company is introducing a new IT programme as part of a package deal. In order to sell the product, Ben needs to attend training with the software designer. Ben has a busy caseload of customers that he currently works with and is struggling to find time to do the training. He is concerned that as the new product is more expensive, his current customers will be closed to any kind of negotiations.

What is the problem here? Ben talks to his Manager about this and his Manager suggests that he takes time to do the training and learn about the new product before he makes his judgement. He tells Ben that the new product is important for business survival and growth as many clients have indicated that the systems are outdated. There are many benefits, and that he should to take the next few days away from the office so that he can complete the training. He encourages Ben to make an action plan and set goals for himself. Ben is to present how he is going to approach this 'change' in a positive way to his Manager, the next morning.

Ben decides to produce a Mind Map to demonstrate this.

Ben presents his mind map to his Manager. Now he has a plan of action he feels ready to face the training.

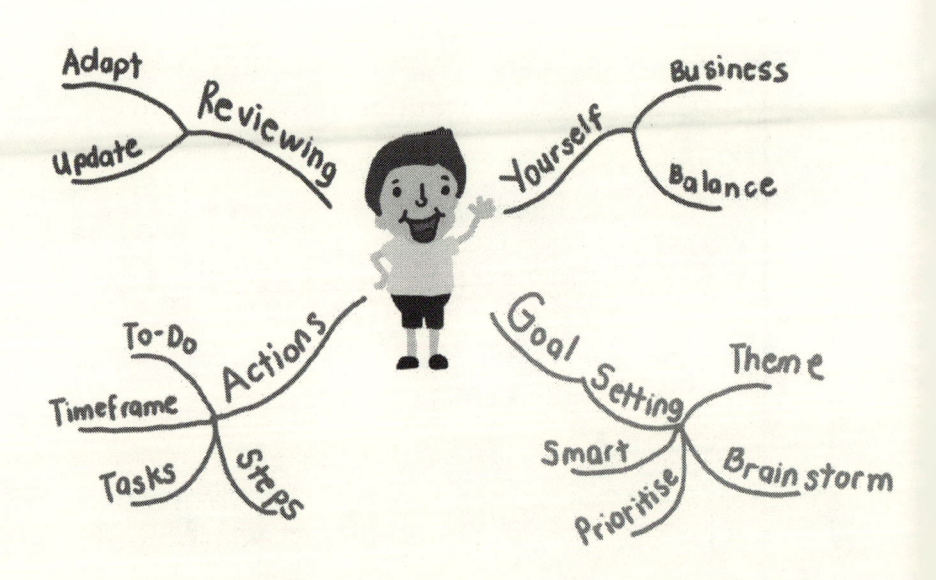

How has creating a mind map helped Ben to embrace the changes?

He approaches the training with an open mind and finds that there are many benefits to the new product and although some of his clients would opt to stick with the current package, there are many unique selling points of the new product that would benefit many of his current clients. He now feels differently about the product and prepares a sales pitch.

Why was Ben so reluctant to embrace change in the beginning?

In summary, Ben was a great IT Consultant, but he was set in his ways. The problem is that Ben didn't see the bigger picture – the change was needed both for the company and its customers too. He already had a large caseload and he probably felt under pressure to learn about the new product.

Luckily for Ben, he had a good Manager who alleviated the pressure by giving him time away from his daily workload so that he could meet the requirements of his job role. Ben used the mind map to make an action plan and alter his mindset in relation to the change.

In truth, if you have a change or problem that seems scary sometimes putting this down on paper in a visual way, can make you realize that the only thing standing in our way, is our self. If we view our problems in a positive way and we can make sense of it on paper, then it's likely that we find a realistic solution. Visual maps can help us to embrace change and solve problems constructively, and in turn, this can make us work in a more effective, efficient and logical way.

How to Improve Time Management & Organization

Do you wish you could manage your own time or be better organized? *Mind maps could be the answer...*

As we discussed earlier in this chapter, it's simple to create a *to-do* list in the form of a mind map, as all you need is a central idea and then your tasks or activities that you need to complete can stem from that. You can use colors to help identify the different subtopic areas and when you've finished, you will be able to see everything you have to do.

At this point, you need to start assessing urgency, importance and timescales, so approach each subtopic/task and ask yourself the following questions:

1. What is the timescale for this task/activity?
2. Is the task urgent?
3. Is the task important?
4. How much time do I need to set aside for this task?

Once you know what you need to do, how long it will take and when you need to complete it, you will be able to start planning and organizing your time. Creating a *to-do* list in this way will help you assess everything you need to do, and it will help you build clarity. You can confidently start working in a productive way because you will have time-based goals, stemming from your mind map.

> **Top Tip**
>
> If you have too many urgent/important tasks, count how many tasks you have in your diagram and number them in order, 1 being the highest priority (both urgent and important). You can then follow the number sequence and complete all tasks in the correct order.

How to Manage Finances with Budgets

Mind mapping concepts can also be used when we create budgets. Budgets can be integral to managing a business or even our personal life. In this section, we will look at examples of both.

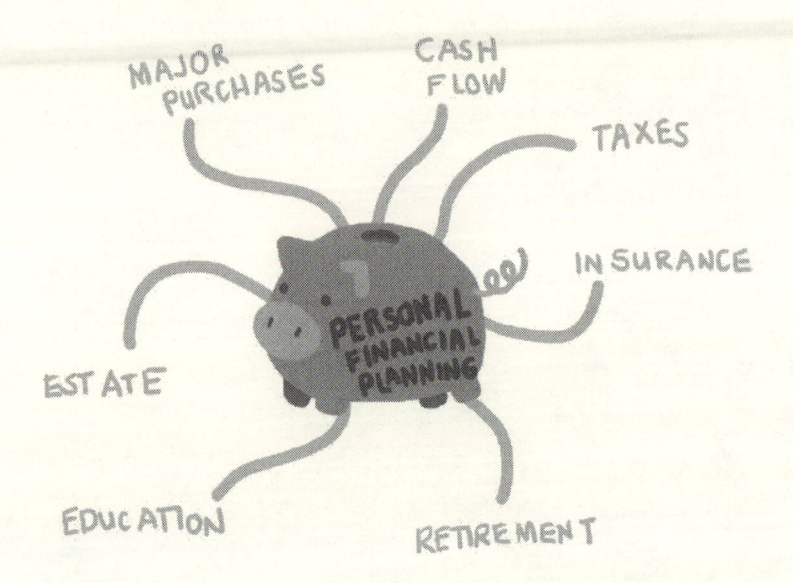

If we are planning a budget, it's important that we know what income and expenditure we have. We also need to project other areas and we might even cap certain spends. For example, if a family needed to save money and found they were paying too much out on food, then they might cap the weekly amount they spend on food shopping.

Sometimes, it becomes apparent that a person or business is trying to spend more than they get in, so planning well allows us to look at the shortfalls, assess how much short we are, can we realistically make this money? If not, what cuts can we make in other areas? If we have a plan of action as well as a back-up plan, then we are less likely to spend overspend. We budget better and are more cautious with our spends when we are aware of the financial situation.

Budgeting in business is built on the same principles, the only difference is that more than one person may work on this. Often in business, collaboration is needed between colleagues or other departments (depending on the business size and structure).

In business, you need to consider staff wages, any other costs like advertising and it can be a much more complex process because there will be more financial priorities and commitments.

Check out the mind map below:

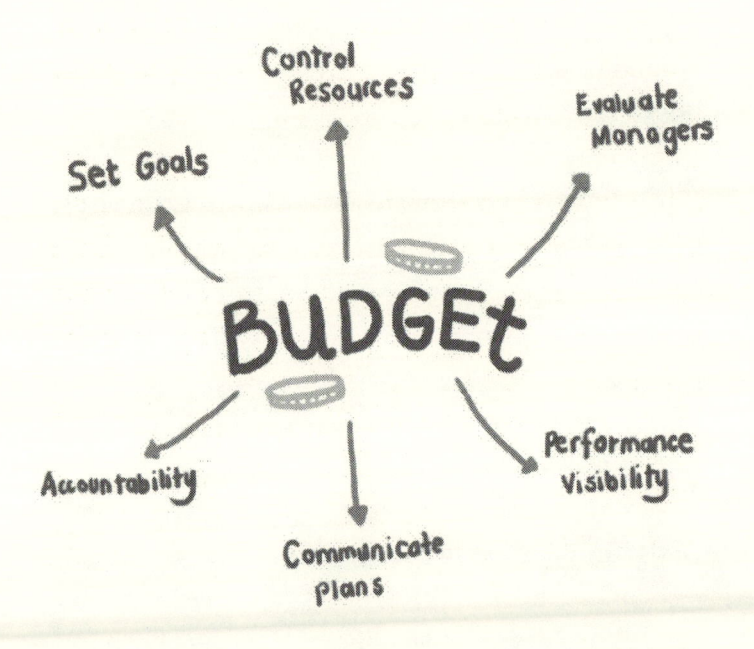

```
        Control
        Resources              Evaluate
Set Goals    ↑                  Managers
       ↖     |                ↙
              BUDGET
       ↙      |        ↘
Accountability |         Performance
               ↓          Visibility
          Communicate
             Plans
```

What differences can you see between a personal budgeting mind map and a business budgeting mind map?

In truth, not a lot, they are just explained in a different way. Also, only you are accountable when it comes to your personal budget but in business, different people may be accountable in different sections or departments of the business.

Business budgets are designed to help us set goals, meet business objectives, prevent our overspends, improve performance and to help us control our resources. Basically, our priorities are different in business and many things focus around business growth, survival and development.

Budgets are just one of the ways we can use a visual map in business. Chapter 14 is wholly about business. In the next chapter, we will look at ways that mind mapping can be used to help us make informed decisions.

9

Mind Mapping for Decision Making

We make decisions on a daily basis. Simple decisions can include deciding what we're going to have for our lunch or whether we are having a bath or shower. In business, we can decide what products and services to offer and we can make significant business decisions. We might need to decide whether to employ a member of staff on a permanent basis or whether to invest in something or not.

In the world we live in, we are faced with many choices. With every choice, we have a decision to make and our choices often impact what happens next. The consequences of our actions can either be positive or negative. We choose our own path in life.

How Do We Make Decisions?

This is an interesting question, because in hindsight, we evaluate the positives and negatives of our choices and choose what we believe will be the best option. Often, that's easier said than done. Of course, we can make simple decisions on a whim using just our mind but if we need to weigh up the positives and negatives to help us decide what we should to.

Mind maps can help with the whole decision-making process and the concept is simple.

Here's how you can customize your visual maps to help you make decisions…

What is your problem? – This is your central idea

What are your solutions/choices? – They are your subcategories.

You can then use your twigs to evaluate your solutions or choices – what are the pros and cons of each? Ask probing questions – who, what, when, where, why and how.

Evaluating Choices with Mind Maps

When you have the completed mind map in front of you, you can start to assess the different choices that you have, and you can really think about the benefits and drawbacks of each different solution. Decisions aren't always easy because there may not be a perfect solution, especially in business. For instance, you may need to decide as to whether you make two staff members redundant or reduce everyone's work hours by 3 hours per week, so that everyone can keep their job. There will be people who can't afford to lose 3 hours pay which means they may seek other employment, but it does mean that everyone keeps their job.

As a mind map is a visual representation, it gives you the opportunity to see things clearly and sometimes, things aren't as bad as they seem.

How to Evaluate Choices

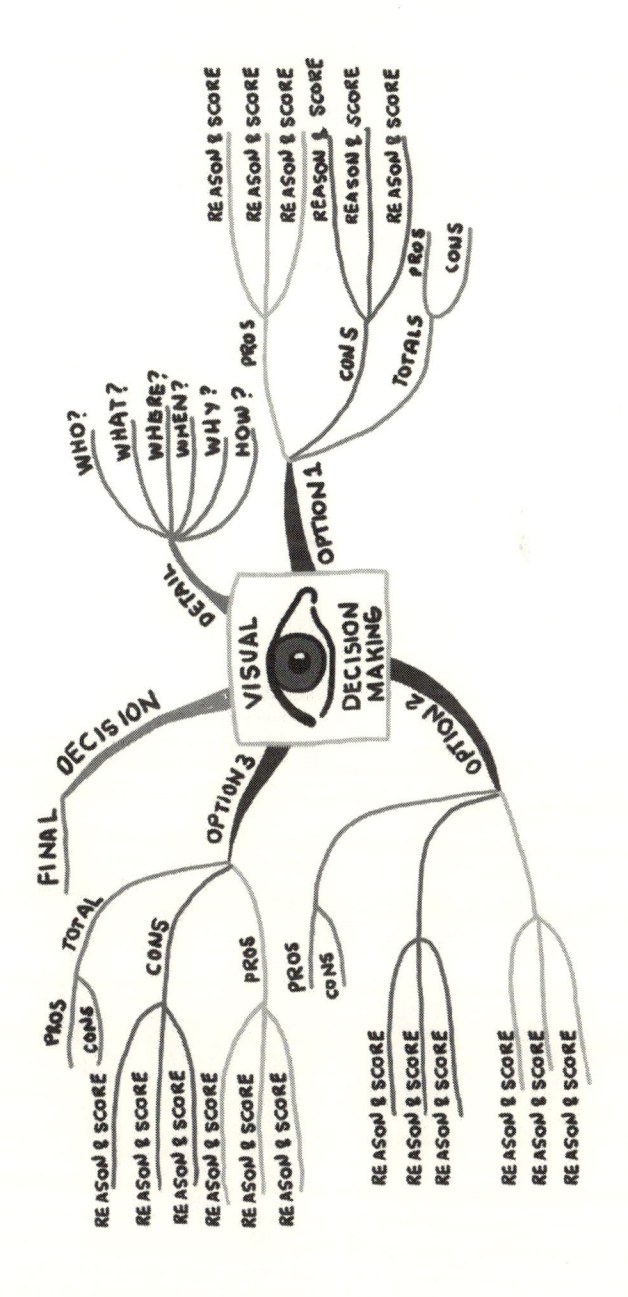

10

Using Mind Maps to Improve Study Methods

Chapter 7 focuses on taking notes, but the purpose of this section is to help you improve your method of notetaking, when you use the mind mapping format. Once you are familiar with the process of using visual maps to take notes, you can start to refine your skills in this art.

How to Take Faster Notes with Mind Maps

There are some things we can focus on if we want to increase the speed of our notetaking. Due to the way that mind maps are designed, we can increase speed without sacrificing quality.

The first thing to do, is ensure that we are clear of the subtopic areas before the notetaking commences. This way we know exactly which section to write our notes, and this means our notes are organized effectively too. If you have an agenda or order of content, then you will be able to write down the names of the different sections before you begin but this isn't always possible as sometimes discussions take us in directions that we don't expect. If you don't have this information, ensure you stick to using one or two words to highlight the name of your subcategory as you may want to change this or merge some subcategories together. You may want to keep a separate section to note down any questions you have but keep them brief by using just a few words.

The second thing to remember when notetaking is 'less is more'. Now, what this essentially means is that you are only going to focus on key words, as they will prompt you when you refer to your notes later. Don't be fooled by this notion, because writing less takes practice as this is hard habit to break.

The third thing to consider, is concentration. Don't worry about making your map look pretty at this stage. Use colors, shapes and images to tidy it up later. When you are taking notes quickly, your most significant job is to get the important words onto the page.

Once you've taken your notes, you can tidy them up. Add colors and shapes, highlight any key points and words. You can even add images too!

How to Study Better with Mind Maps

Mind maps are an effective study tool because they are visually appealing with their curved branches, colors and shapes. They link relevant points together which means your thoughts are more organized and this allows us to process information in a quick and efficient way. The fact that they are made up of key words and there is minimal information, means that your brain is prompted to think freely and creatively.

7 WAYS TO IMPROVE YOUR GRAMMAR
- KNOW
- STUDY
- READ
- SPELL CHECK
- ACTIVE VERBS
- PRACTICE

If you want to study better, there are many different types of mind maps that we have looked at already that will be beneficial to you.

Brainstorming is discussed in chapter 5 and it's a great way to expand and explore your ideas. In chapter 6, we talk about using visual maps to plan your writing. In chapter 7, we talk about using maps when notetaking and in chapter 8, we talk about using mind maps when planning. In this chapter, we have already discussed, speed when notetaking, planning and organizing our time effectively, as well as goal setting.

All these mind mapping methods that we've covered will help you to study, but how can we learn to study better with mind maps?

> **Five tips to help you improve your studies, when using mind maps:**
>
> **Tip 1**- Mind maps are meant to be a visual learning and planning tool, so use them in the way that they are intended. Once you've finished, you can use shapes, colors and images to tidy up your notes.
>
> **Tip 2** - Review your notes by looking over your completed map, one section at a time. Notice how the categories and subcategories link together and give your brain time to absorb the information.
>
> **Tip 3** - Implement your map by turning it into a more detailed plan. Mind maps are just the beginning of your project and they can prompt you to take further action. If you are planning your time or organizing yourself, you may turn this into a schedule

or calendar, for calendar blocking. If this is a plan of your novel, then you may write your chapter outlines from your diagram.

Tip 4 - Analyze each subcategory and note down relevant questions that you need to know or answer. You can then go off and research the relevant areas.

Tip 5 - Use your mind map for revision. It can be used as a great revision cramming session. You can reflect on the key words and check that you've remembered vital points as well as answering any questions you've posed.

Recommendations: Future Chapters That Will Enhance your Study Skills

The following chapters may also be useful if you want to improve your studying skills.

Chapter 11, Mind Mapping for Mindset – to help you get in the right mindset when you're studying.

Chapter 12, How to Recall Information – to help you use mind maps in the most effective way to help you remember key information.

Chapter 15, Mind Mapping for Problem Solving – will help you answer and explain solutions to problems you encounter. Problem solving is a key tool that is applicable to everyday life, studying and learning, and it can also be used in business.

Chapter 16, Mind Mapping for Learning New Languages – will demonstrate how mind mapping techniques can be used to enhance learning new skills, such as a language. The concept can be used when studying.

11

Mind Mapping for Mindset

Mindset is a very insightful topic because it can be the key as to whether you succeed in life. Mindset is an attitude; it's a way that we feel and act – it's where we are in our own head space.

If you have a positive mindset, you can achieve anything. You have self-esteem, confidence and an optimistic outlook. These three things fuel your mindset and in turn, drive your motivation. If we do not have the right outlook, it can be hard to achieve anything at all.

Your mindset mind map should be a visual representation of you!

If you aren't in the right frame of mind, you may need to explore what you need to do to change this. It can be difficult if you have low self-esteem, confidence and motivation issues as we may struggle to know our purpose.

How to Find Purpose

In order to find a purpose, you need to dig deep, and you need to be ready to accept the negative and the positive aspects of yourself.

This requires some research, so ask some of your trustworthy friends and family members:

- What do I do well?
- What do I need to do better?
- If you need some advice, what would you come to me for?
- What do you see me doing in five years' time?
- What three characteristics would you use to describe me?

This is how other people see you!

Personal exploration is also important. Subsequently, you should ask yourself:

- What am I good at?
- What should I improve on?
- What are my life goals, or what do I want (It can be more than one thing)?
- Why do I want it?
- When do I want it?
- How and/or where am I going to get it?

You could answer these using the brainstorming method.

Once you know more about what you are good at (confirmed by yourself and others) you can start to think about a purpose – think about why you want, what you want? Why do you deserve it?

Well done, you're starting to consider your own purpose!

Now, turn these into goals – ensure they are S.M.A.R.T.

How to Achieve your Goals!

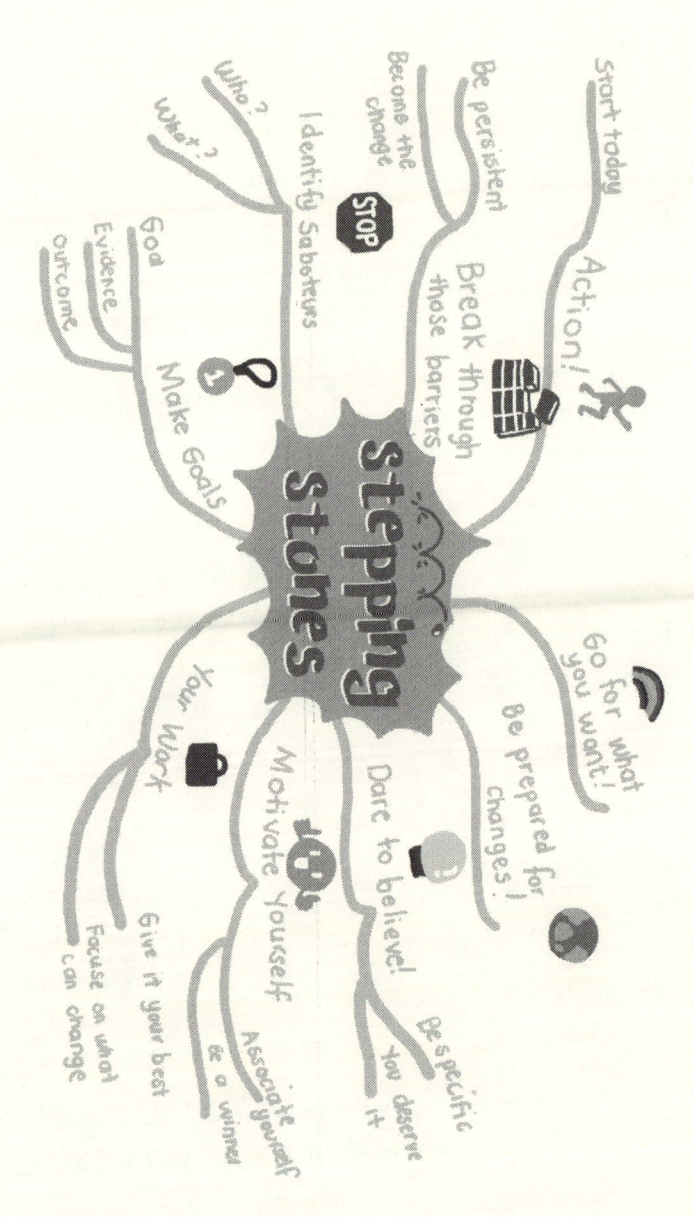

How to Visualize Your Life Goals

First of all, you should consider why we visualize our life goals. Earlier in this chapter, we discussed using mind maps in the essence that they were produced for, and we established that this is essentially a visual learning and planning tool. If you visualize your goals, it gives you the opportunity to imagine what life would be like if you achieved those goals and you can see the bigger picture. Ask yourself, what are the benefits of achieving my life goals?

Look at your goals. Picture them. Think about the result and your journey to achieving your goal – what is your ideal scenario if you achieve that goal? If we know what the benefits are, how can we achieve our goals? Often if we can see that our hopes or dreams are within our grasp, then we will feel more motivated and driven towards achieving them. THIS is what you are aiming for!

After you note down what you want to achieve, you feel a sense of relief because you've just emptied your head, onto paper. Once you've turned them into goals, they become memorable.

Seeing your goals visually, is a powerful reminder of what we want to achieve, and this can give us a sense of motivation. Remember that your goals should be S.M.A.R.T and you should think about how you can achieve this – visualize it. Use colors, shapes, curved lines and images to make it more appealing. Visualize the result and reap the benefits!

Once you have a clear and inspirational mind map, it will stay in your brain as you will remember it. Pin it up so that you can see it every day and you'll remember what you are working towards. Just the very sight of it will trigger motivation in your head.

Don't forget that motivation is a mindset!

Crafting your Ideal Future

If you're working on crafting your ideal future, creating a mind map to alter mindsets (as we've discussed above) is a great start, but how can we begin to craft our future based on that?

Imagine your ideal future… Think about personal life, business or work, your health, and what makes you happy. *What do you really want in relation to those things?*

You now know your purpose and what you are good at and you've written down your life goals.

Basically, you have a visual representation of your future life – it's within your grasp.

How are you going to make it happen?

This isn't an instant process so don't expect miracles. Being motivated is only the first step, because you also must be accountable for your life goals too. As human beings, we are programmed 'to go and get' the things we need to survive. If we are hungry, we do whatever we need to do, to eat. This is a basic need that we need to meet in order to survive. We don't roll over and give up if we can't be bothered to get something to eat as survival mode kicks in, and we go and get what we want, or what we need.

You now feel motivated, right? So, you need to view your ideal future and life goals, in the same way that you view your basic needs. You need to go and get it, because your survival depends on it!

Sounds extreme, doesn't it? If you are in the right frame of mind and you NEED to achieve your life goals, then you will go and get it. If you don't view it in that way, then you may never achieve it. That's not to suggest that everything will go according to plan for you, as there may hit barriers from time to time. If it takes longer than anticipated to reach your goals, that's okay. If you can maintain that motivation by achieving some short-term goals, you will see the steady progress and know that you are heading in the right direction. Acceptance is vital here.

Top Tips to when Crafting your Ideal Future:

1. Use the mind map strategies that we've discussed to construct your goals.
2. Your ideal future is now a basic need – keep focusing on what you have to gain by achieving this. Nothing can stop you!
3. Form plans, S.M.A.R.T goals and objectives so that you know exactly what you're aiming for.
4. Allow space in your calendar and schedule time to work on your goals.
5. Use your mind maps to help you visualize your goals (why not produce a vision board to reinforce your life goals?).
6. Visualize your life goals every day and remember that feeling – the one you feel when you imagine yourself there.
7. Create a to-do list to co-exist with your goals and tick off your progress as you work

through them. This will help you to see and celebrate your progress.
8. Don't give up – even if you have to adapt or change your goals, or if they take longer to achieve. Maintain your concentration and stay motivated until you make steady progress.

Finally, it's important to remember that sometimes our hopes, wants and dreams change and that's okay. If you had a life goal to move to New York 6 years ago, but since then you've had children and started a family, and you now share the dream to live in Australia with your partner, just change your goal. It's important not to change your goals because you feel defeated, but if you genuinely want something else instead, go ahead. Visualize a new plan!

12

How to Recall Information

Do you have a good memory or a bad memory?

Many people talk about memory as if it is simply good or bad, as if we are born with either one or the other, but that is not necessarily the case. Scientists believe that different techniques can be used to help our memory develop as they think of memory as a skill. While this is possible in most cases, we obviously shouldn't ignore that there are health conditions or injuries that can damage our memory and its capacity, however, the memory is a wonderful thing that stores, remembers and retains lots of information.

It is possible to train our memory and practice our recall skills to improve our memory. *Have you ever listened to a song or sound that has brought back a memory?* Pictures and words can prompt us in exactly the same way. This is why mind maps have proved an effective tool to help us recall information. [15]

In order to use our memory effectively, we should keep it healthy. It is suggested that in order to keep a healthy mind, we should:

- ✓ Eat good food and stay hydrated.
- ✓ Ensure we get enough sleep/rest.
- ✓ Use different learning techniques. In this section we will explore many different learning techniques that we can use alongside our mind map to help with your learning.
- ✓ It's important to keep your memory active. We can practice remembering and recalling information as if you regularly practice these skills, you will expand your mind and it will become stronger.
- ✓ Healthy competition is good for the mind too. Compete against others and strive to win. Try to use all 5 senses to keep your mind in a heightened state. [16]

Now, we can explore how mind maps can be a useful aid as a prompt to help you thrive and grow.

How to Remember Better

Visual learners learn by seeing. They are learners who review graphics and images. The more appealing you make the visual, the more it sticks in their mind. For a visual learner, less is more, and it prompts them to remember facts and nuggets of information. Consider word-picture association prompts for instance. If we are learning a new language or even new words as a child, we can be shown flashcards. Once the word is learned alongside the picture (often through repetition) simply showing the picture would prompt us to say the word. Every time we review the picture, we would then say the word. That's because the picture is visually appealing, and it sticks in your mind. We remember it by associating a picture with a word.

Mind maps are perfect for the visual learner, because we use images and key words as part of a diagram with flowing lines and plenty of colors to help us organize the thoughts in our mind. The diagram itself acts as a prompt.

How to Remember Names

To use mind maps to remember names, you still need to have a central idea, and this obviously depends on exactly what names you are trying to remember and what this means to you.

For example, if you want to recall members of your family, you can use the mind mapping functions to create a family tree.

131

You might want to remember a series of people in your life, so your central idea may be focused on people in your life, and then your subcategories could be work/college/school, family, friends, neighbors, associates, and then from that, you would extend further and list their names.

If you want to remember names for study purposes, let's say character names, then you might set out your mind maps in the same way as the adjacent example:

This image is looking at characters in William Shakespeare's *Romeo and Juliet*. We've already mentioned just how powerful a mind map can be as a learning tool, but this can really help a person remember characters, their name, and who they are linked to/their importance.

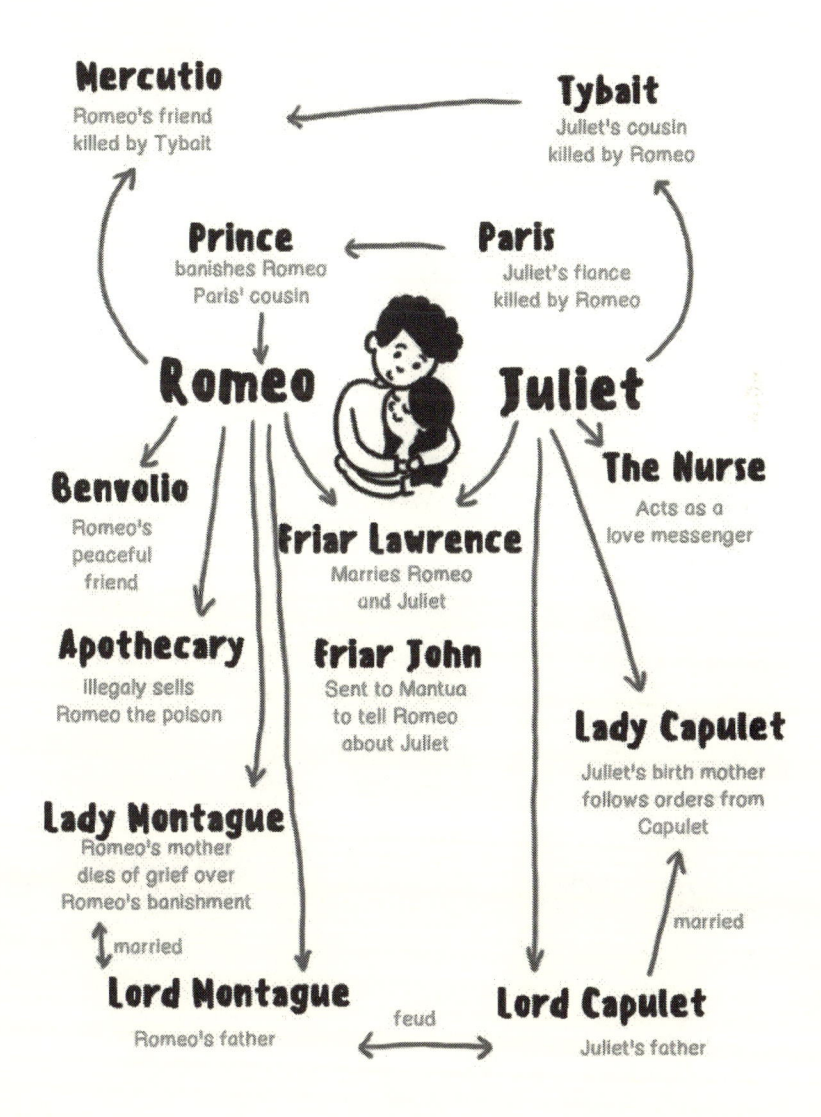

Mercutio — Romeo's friend killed by Tybalt

Tybalt — Juliet's cousin killed by Romeo

Prince — banishes Romeo, Paris' cousin

Paris — Juliet's fiance killed by Romeo

Romeo

Juliet

Benvolio — Romeo's peaceful friend

Friar Lawrence — Marries Romeo and Juliet

The Nurse — Acts as a love messenger

Apothecary — illegally sells Romeo the poison

Friar John — Sent to Mantua to tell Romeo about Juliet

Lady Capulet — Juliet's birth mother follows orders from Capulet

Lady Montague — Romeo's mother dies of grief over Romeo's banishment

married

Lord Montague — Romeo's father

feud

Lord Capulet — Juliet's father

married

You may even choose images when mind mapping or you could use a combination of images and words like the example below:

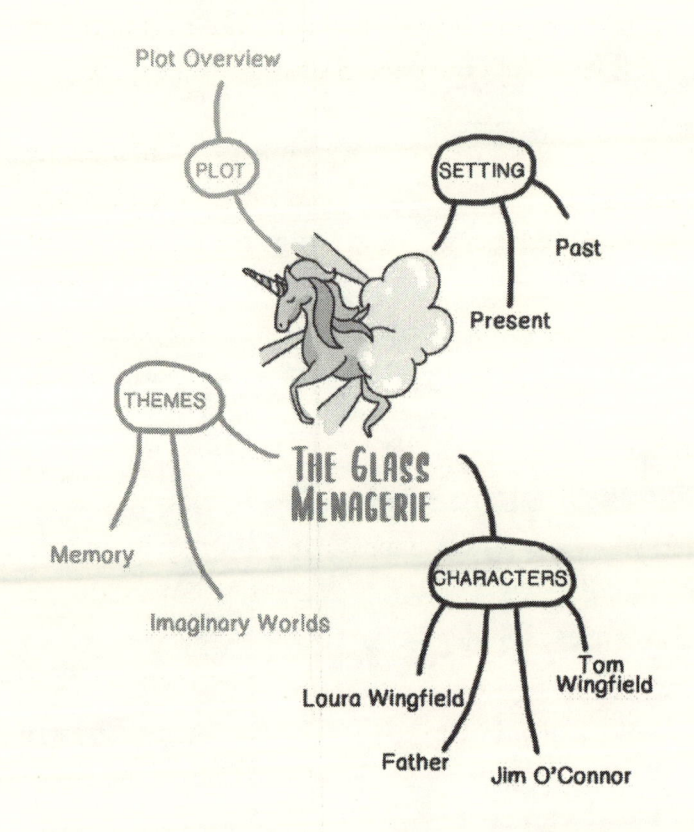

Plot Overview

- PLOT
- SETTING
  - Past
  - Present
- THEMES
  - Memory
  - Imaginary Worlds
- THE GLASS MENAGERIE
- CHARACTERS
  - Laura Wingfield
  - Tom Wingfield
  - Father
  - Jim O'Connor

The most important here is to find the best way to mind map, that is right for you, personally. It's there to benefit you, so if you prefer images, use images.

Although the way you set out your mind map is an integral part when you're trying to remember names, ensure that the format suits you and you can make sense of it. If you haven't already realized, visual maps are flexible and should be displayed in a way that suits the person who creates or uses it.

The next stage of remembering names is visualizing. Visualizing is an important technique to prompt our memory and therefore it's important to use images, colors and curved lines. The more visually appealing the map is, the more likely you are to remember. Follow the steps below when visualizing names:

1. Find a quiet space so that you can concentrate.
2. Look closely at your diagram. Study it. Follow the curves of every line and take notice of the words and images.
3. Sit down and close your eyes and imagine the image in your mind.
4. If you are using key words, visualize the name and turn the word into a picture.
5. If you are using an image, then visualize the picture and imagine the name alongside this too.
6. Review the spelling of the name and run carefully through each letter. Say the letters aloud and visualize them in a familiar place.

Maybe they are magnets and twirl in turn, landing on a magnetic board. Remember, this visualization technique is for you individually, so allow yourself to be creative and think freely.

7. Associate the image with the word. After all of the letters are in place, the accompanying image of the person arrives too. Really focus on this and what they look like.
8. Concentrate on one particular feature of the person – what do you notice about their appearance? What's unusual?
9. Another useful visualization technique is to think of silly or crazy you associate with that person. Maybe you can think about the person doing something silly or associate something else when thinking of their name. Allow yourself to use your imagination and be creative – this is your memory prompt!
10. Link your names together. Who is with the person you first visualized? Visualize them together, then focus on the new person and repeat the steps again and again. The pace of your visualization should quicken as you imagine the people linked together.
11. Group them together – once you have around 5 people visualized; you need to store them in your memory. Create a room in your mind to store your 'people'. This is a term often referred to as a *Memory Palace*. A Memory Palace

is a memory enhancement technique from ancient Roman and Greek times, that looks at visualization techniques that utilizes spatial memory. Links are made between the things we need to remember and information that is already familiar to us so that we can recall information quickly. Imagine all 5 people in that room, doing the thing that makes them unique. Focus in on each person in turn. Imagine their name and their unique feature. Then move on to the next 5 names and repeat the process. When you return to your room, with the next 5, you need to attempt to recall all 10 names, and then 15 names after you work on the next 5. It's important to keep recalling and refreshing the previous names you've learned throughout the whole learning process. [17]

How to Remember Facts

Mind maps are great if you want to remember facts. Create your mind map around a central idea and then use key words within subcategories based on your central idea. Your key words should work as a prompt, so that you remember a specific fact.

Once you have your completed diagram, you're ready to start memorizing your facts.

You should start doing this by studying your mind map and visualizing your key words. Focus on one word at a time and visualize the word and it's spelling. Don't forget to close your eyes! Think about the fact this represents and repeat this aloud.

You can use images too, if this works best for you. If you find it does, use the methods discussed above in the *How to Remember Names* section. Visualize your key words alongside your image and repeat the fact that you need to remember aloud.

When you've practiced learning your facts you need to embed them into your mind.

An effective method to use when remembering and recalling is a technique called *spaced repetition*. This is when you space out the time in between your learning practice. To use spaced repetition to remember facts, you should visualize your key word and fact. You then move onto the next fact and group them together again; 5 is a great number. You can then use spaced repetition to recall the 5 facts. Then have a break from this, by reviewing the next 5 facts. You can then practice your first 5 facts and the next 5 facts together, until you can recall all facts, using your visualization techniques and key word prompts. [18]

Have you heard the saying that practice makes perfect? This couldn't be a truer term. After you have spent time rehearsing and repeating your facts, you should then spend time recalling them as this will challenge your learning capacity. Increasing the time in between recalling your learned information is known as spaced retrieval. If you can return to your map the next day and recall your facts easily using your visualization techniques, then you know that you are beginning to embed these facts into your mind. It means that you have learned these, effectively. [19]

How to Remember Lost Items

Is it even possible to use mind maps to remember lost items? In short, the answer is yes. Mind maps can be effective when we are trying to remember lost items because they help us to expand our mind, focus and think clearly.

When you lose something, it's usually because you've switched into auto pilot mode. This is where you have lots on your mind or maybe you're even tired or distracted. You are in a subconscious state and you might automatically put something in a place that is familiar to you, however, you may not remember where this is, and you will not recall putting the item there either. It's a strange feeling, because we wrack our brains and we can't think clearly, because we are unable to recall.

There are three possible ways we can deal with this:

First, we can train ourselves to put items in a particular place by adopting a routine. This way, when we do switch into a robotic state, we mindlessly put the item into the correct place.

If it's too late for that and you've already lost your item, you can use some memory retrieval techniques to help you find your missing item. It's common to misplace things like keys or mobile phones. Take yourself off to a quiet place and close your eyes. Try visualizing your day or the last time you had the item you're searching for. You should then move through the events that follow this and think about the last thing you remember before you lost your item. Often this will prompt you to search in a few places and sometimes you will retrieve the item easily.

If you still aren't sure, then you should make a visual map to help you investigate further.

Where was I?

Who did I see?

Where have I been?

LOST KEYS

Where was I?

When did I last see it?

The lost item is your central idea – you should use an image to represent this. You should then map out the day as your subcategories (where you have been, possible places you could have put your item based on that, think about who was there, places you usually put your item too. Use twigs from the subcategories to list your key words. Once you've emptied your brain onto the page, tidy it up by using colors for your branches and subcategories. Take a few deep breaths and try to clear your mind. Study your diagram by looking at each sub-category in turn and focus on the key words. Then use visualization techniques to imagine the key words. Visualize your item in your mind too and see if you can make any links to where the item might be. Hopefully you will be prompted to look in the right places for your item.

Obviously, it isn't guaranteed that you will find your item. Your mind must have already absorbed and processed the memory subconsciously in order for you to remember. There are occasions when this hasn't happened and recalling this information isn't possible.

Improving your memory and maintaining a healthy mind is key to recalling information. Although mind maps can be an effective tool for recall, ultimately getting into a routine and expanding your mind is a useful preventative technique to prevent the loss in the first place.

13

Mind Mapping for Creativity

We've already talked about the creativity and free-thinking that is encouraged when using visual maps. Mind mapping techniques are great for sparking and developing our creativity. They encourage us to explore new ideas that under normal circumstances we may brush under the carpet or ignore.

Why is that?

To put it simply, there is an important philosophy that we should adopt if we want mind mapping to work, and that's to have a non-judgmental approach because every idea we have, matters. Regardless of how wild or extravagant they are, they count, and we need to acknowledge them because these visual aids help us to open our minds, develop ourselves and others, as well as unleashing our creativity and innovation.

Leadership with Mind Maps

An effective leader has strong communication skills and always listens to staff members. They are professional, yet open to innovation and new ideas. They encourage their staff and have a positive, yet professional approach. They encourage forward-thinking and most of all, they make each and every staff member feels valued.

Visuals are great tools for leaders. In this book already, we've already discussed how we can use mind maps to:

- ✓ **Set goals and objectives.** We can easily set goals and objectives for our team, and we can also help them set personal development goals.
- ✓ **Take notes at lectures and seminars.** If the team manager had been to a

management meeting, they could explain relevant aspects of the meeting to staff members by using the notes they've taken, and they can present them in the form of a visual map.
- ✓ **Brainstorm ideas.** You can adopt brainstorming techniques at team meetings to help your colleagues solve problems, or you can grow our ideas on products, services and working methods.
- ✓ **Make decisions.** Mind mapping the pros and cons of an idea can help us to make business decisions. It can also help our staff or team members understand why we made a certain business decision in the first place.
- ✓ **Alter mindsets.** We know that we can use maps to alter the mindset of ourselves, and we can also use them to alter our team's mindset too.

We already know we can use all the mind map variations above can help us to be an effective leader. Mind maps not only help us to make sense of our thoughts, they can also help us to display our thoughts in a way that others understand too.

If we are a leader and we oversee other staff members, mind mapping techniques can be invaluable. We can put the on display to remind

145

staff expected behaviors, establish rules, detail team goals for the week, plan meetings, and any positive quotes or affirmations for the week. If we complete appraisals, supervisions or performance reviews we can use visual maps to plan out future training and progression for our staff members.

There's no doubt that an effective leader should lead by example. Mind maps are motivational tools that can inspire creativity and forward-thinking. If you incorporate them when leading others, it can create an environment of openness and your staff will improve their performance as they will feel valued, especially if they feel that their ideas and needs are considered.

WORK SMART

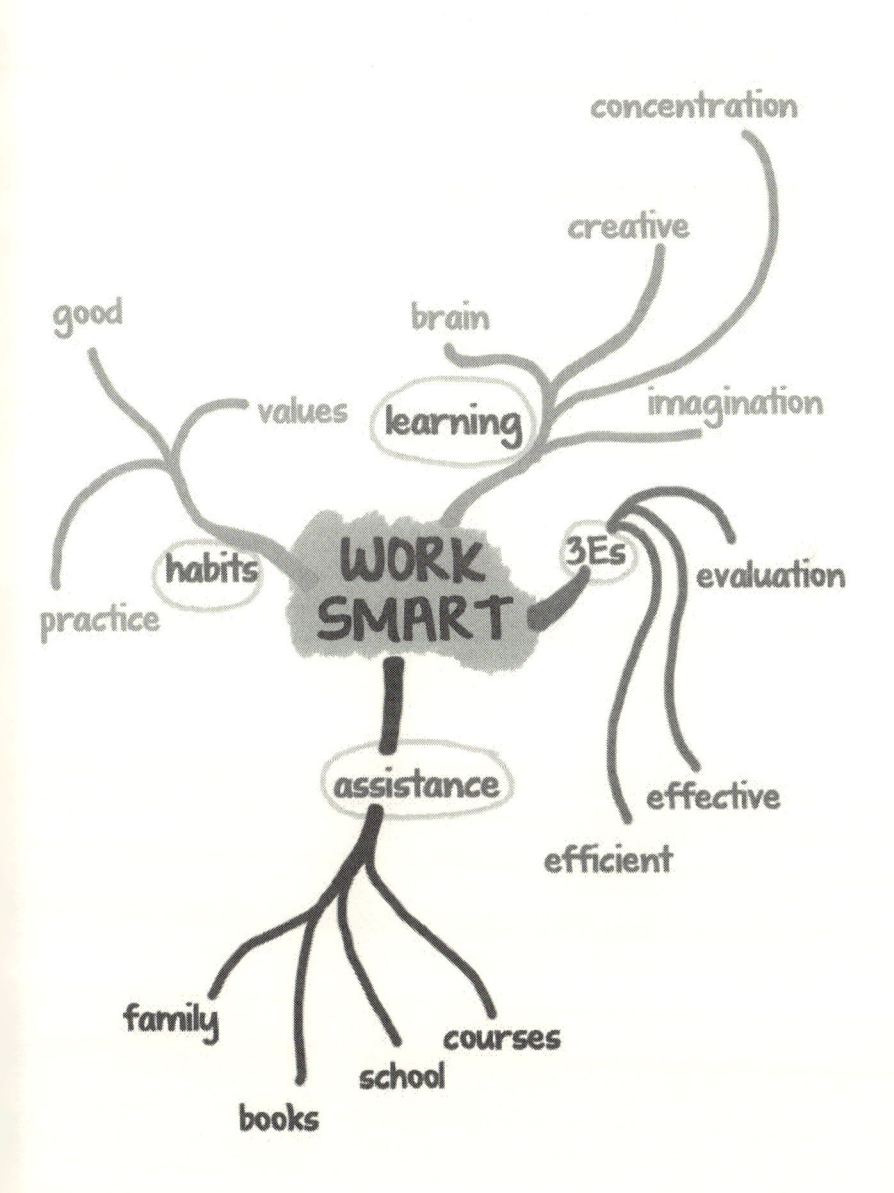

- **learning**
  - brain
  - creative
  - concentration
  - imagination
- **habits**
  - good
  - values
  - practice
- **3Es**
  - evaluation
  - effective
  - efficient
- **assistance**
  - family
  - books
  - school
  - courses

How to Promote Idea Generation (Free Thinking) and Innovation

Mind mapping is a great tool if we want to generate ideas, encourage free or forward thinking, and promote innovation.

If you want to generate ideas and free thinking, you should use the Brainstorming mind mapping techniques covered in *Chapter 5: Brainstorming with mind maps*.

Brainstorms don't have to be individual. If you are facilitating a group, you could ask people to work in pairs or small groups, and then when you've all completed the activity, you could collect all ideas on one large board or flipchart sheet. Some will be the same, but others will be different, and this might spark the creativity of the rest of the group.

To push ideas further you should create your own probing questions, based on the questioning techniques we discussed in the earlier chapters, that start with:

- Who?
- What?
- When?

- Where?
- Why?
- How?

Remember, when mind mapping, especially when you're in a group, ensure you instill the notion that every idea and person in the group should be valued and respected, and everyone is expected to participate.

Providing you promote the right atmosphere, success and creativeness will occur as you will generate the 'idea bouncing' effect. This is when one person has an idea, that prompts a further idea from another person. Ideas bounce from person to person, and as that idea grows, it strengthens. This can build confidence and motivation within a group setting as each person agrees and clarifies the idea of the previous person. It's a validation process.

Mind Mapping for Strategic Thinking

Strategic thinking is a serious subject, right? If we are a leader or want to progress and develop in business, we need to be able to think strategically.

What do we mean 'Strategic Thinking'?

The term strategic is closely linked to strategy. If we have a strategy, then basically, we have a plan. Strategic is a term that we usually refer to in the world of business and it's often something that higher management is involved in. The truth is, the word strategic sounds scarier than it is. To think strategically, you need to focus on a goal or objective and then plan how you will achieve this.

150

It's not exactly the same, as the 'strategic' part is down to the clever planning we do in order to achieve the thing we are aiming for. For our plan to be strategic, it needs to be calculated and well-thought out.

In Chapter 8, we use mind maps to create SMART goals and objectives. If you can do this, you're on your way to strategic bliss. You are taking your goal or objective to the next level. Your goal or objective is the result you want to achieve but you need a calculated plan to get there and you need to really focus on your goal to make your strategy, infallible. If something is strategic, it's planned in a way that is unlikely to fail because it's planned so well – almost fail-safe. Of course, this is not a guarantee, but that's the general idea.

Let's find out how we can take our goals or objectives to the next level…

Your goal or objective is your central idea. You will then break down your goal into subcategory areas by questioning yourself. Really visualize the transformation you want to achieve here – where are you/is the business now, and where should it be? Really reflect on the journey of this transformation.

When completing your visual map, you need to think about the tactics you can use, the strengths and weaknesses/pros and cons, think about the purpose, quality and value, and visualize your end goal/objectives and how you will get there.

Use the questions we discussed in earlier units – who, what, when, where, why and how. Also, think about what problems you may encounter and how you will solve them. It's important to allow your free thinking and creativity to flow here too. Some of the best ideas come to us out of the blue, when we're thinking creatively.

Don't expect your first mind map to be perfect. Thinking strategically is quite complex and we must train ourselves to think outside the box. We could further explore ideas from this too by researching topics further, as we may need to make key business decisions, based on this strategic planning.

Once you've completed your mind map, you have the opportunity to study it and work out the methods that work best. You will be able to use your key ideas to write up your planning report that details how you can achieve your goal in an effective and efficient way.

Think about how you can adopt this method!

14

Mind Mapping for Business & Work Performance

Mind maps are a common tool used in business. That is because if a business wants to move with the times and push for innovation, they are a great planning tool that promotes creative and forward thinking. Mind mapping is commonly used for brainstorming meetings, to plan projects and to forecast a strategy for growth, to name a few. We've also explored some of these in previous chapters, but they can be used for so much more and in this chapter, we are going to explore how we can use them for effective business practice.

Estimating Project Timelines

Mind maps are a great way to plan your estimated project timelines. Now, we already know how to create a robust visual map, but in order to tailor this to meet your needs, we must consider the format.

When it comes to estimating project timelines, it means that the first stages of your projects are already planned out and you will know the steps you need to follow. This means that you can quite confidently use the name of the project in the center, as this is your central idea.

Following on from that, your first subcategories will be the steps you need to follow to complete your project (they will usually be objectives). You then need to smaller branches to break down your objectives into smaller tasks.

Now the initial stage of your mind map is complete, so now you can work to tidy this up and you should consider the following:

- Look at your subcategories that stem from your central idea and consider them carefully. Number them in a logical order (for instance, number 1 might be the objective that should be completed first).

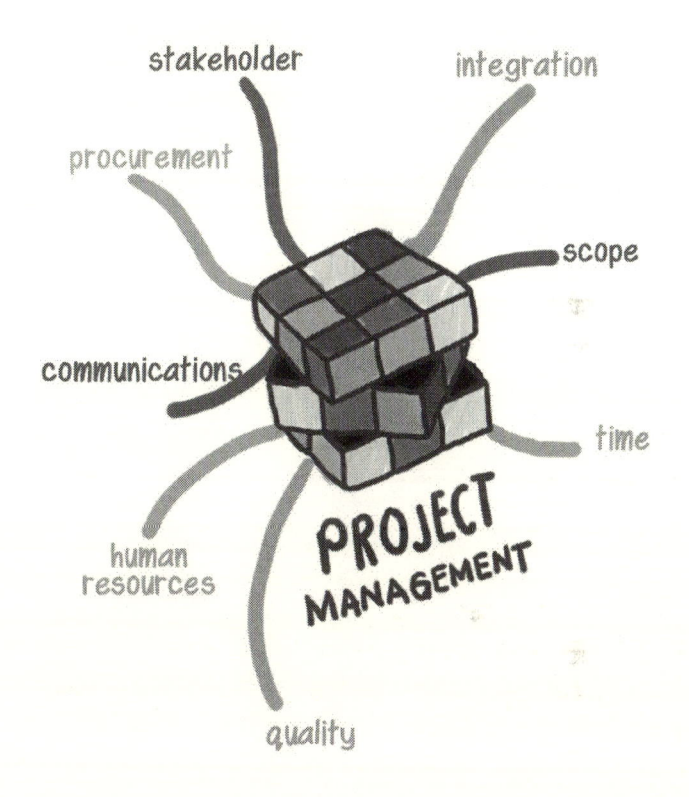

stakeholder

integration

procurement

scope

communications

time

human resources

PROJECT MANAGEMENT

quality

- Look at the smaller tasks that break down each of your objectives and attach a timescale to each of these. Remember that when you plan a timescale, you need to be generous and realistic. If they are too tight, then you have less chance of achieving them and this can affect motivation.

- You can then customize the plan to meet your needs – add up the timescales so that you know the whole time it will take to complete each of your objectives/steps.
- Once all your times are planned and you know the date your project is starting, you can start to plan actual dates of completion for each objective. Once you've planned to this level, you will be able to forecast an end date for the whole project.

Preparing for Negotiations

Negotiation is an important tool in business. It's a great way to settle differences but there are many stages to negotiation. First you should prepare, and then you need to discuss with the relevant parties. It's then a good idea to set goals, before you negotiate your outcome. Of course, you should come to an agreement before you implement the actionable steps you must take.

Diagrams are great for the initial planning stage. If you have a goal or something you want to achieve in business that involves other companies or colleagues, you may need to negotiate. Whenever change is a possibility, it's important to demonstrate strong negotiation skills. Again, mind mapping for negotiations is the same concept as regular mind mapping, but we have to organize it differently. When you are negotiating you need to be able to anticipate and address both sides of an argument and problem solve anything that stands in your way of achieving your goal.

Start with your central idea, in the center of your diagram and then your subcategories should focus on the different people/groups/companies that you will need to negotiate with. If it's a group of people, you should consider key roles/relationships within the group, so you know who the biggest influence is when decision making.

Once you know *who* you're negotiating with, you can start to branch off further and think about *what* it is that you're negotiating. What might you need to negotiate with the people in your subcategories? What might they have a problem with?

When you know the *who and what*, you can think about why and how. If you know why they might have a problem or how to solve it, it becomes likely that you will be able to anticipate a solution. For instance, if there is a cost increase to a product or service, in the first instance you would explain your reasons for the increase. You can then think about why they would have a problem with a price increase. For every reason, *why*, you should think of an answer. Negotiating requires an element of problem solving so once your visual map is complete, you can start to examine it. *How can you flip this?* Nobody likes a price increase, but maybe you could offer long-term customers a slight discount (set yourself boundaries if you are considering this), or maybe you can explain exactly what they are paying for and reiterate why the increase is necessary in the first place.

Once you've prepared for this negotiation, you can use the mind map to guide you through your discussion phase. Think about what you want to achieve from this negotiation. You can also set personal or business goals using visual maps to enhance this process, as we discussed in Chapter 8.

How to Create Successful Presentations

As we've discussed several times throughout this book, a mind map is a great visual tool to display a vision or idea, as well as being a great planning tool.

There are two functions to a visual map when creating a successful presentation. First, you could use a mind map to actually plan your presentation. Put the title of your presentation or presentation topic idea in the center, then build on the different slides – *how many slides will you have?* They will be your subcategories, then use key words to indicate the content of each slide. You can then build a well-planned presentation from this.

If you are presenting to a group of people, you can make things clear and visually appealing with imagery. You could create a mind map that highlights business growth, to show a new product, or even to display different income streams for the business and how they are performing.

Often visual representations make things clearer for the audience as it allows them to absorb, process and understand key points of information easily. If you choose to include a mind map within your presentation, then you need to make it as appealing as possible, if you want to ensure success.

In Chapter 4, we looked at organizing your mind map and using colors to highlight the different areas and this is important if you are presenting your map others. It would be advised to make a rough draft copy first, before you create the diagram within your presentation. You can include this as a picture or there are tools and symbols available to create the mind map within the presentation software. Remember you can use images as part of your mind map too, so just ensure that it's as clear and as visually appealing as possible, for maximum impact.

How to Create a Successful Presentation

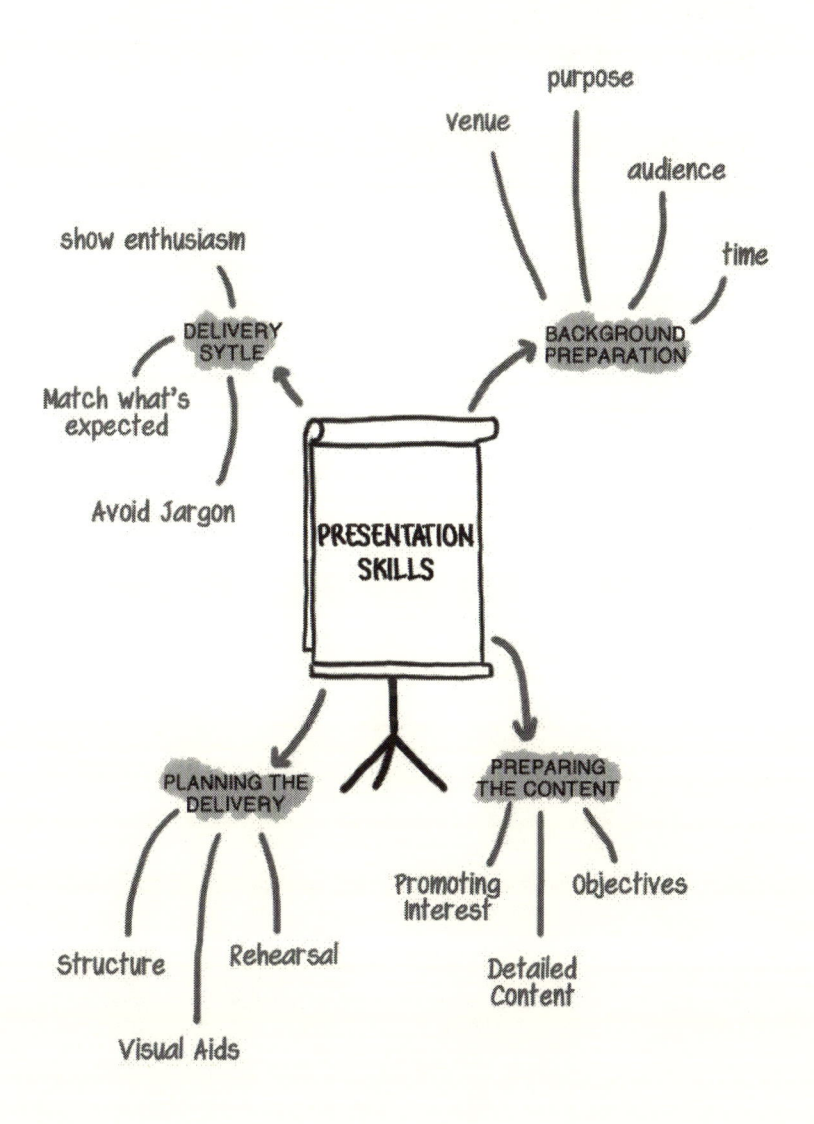

PRESENTATION SKILLS

- **BACKGROUND PREPARATION**
  - venue
  - purpose
  - audience
  - time

- **DELIVERY SYTLE**
  - show enthusiasm
  - Match what's expected
  - Avoid Jargon

- **PLANNING THE DELIVERY**
  - Structure
  - Rehearsal
  - Visual Aids

- **PREPARING THE CONTENT**
  - Promoting Interest
  - Objectives
  - Detailed Content

Mind Mapping for Effective Management

There's no reason why we can't use a mind map for effective management. They have endless benefits which includes helping to plan, organize and set goals. In the previous chapter, we looked at how we can use them for leadership, so you can also refer to Chapter 13 too if you want to know how you can become an effective leader.

Mind mapping can be a great way to grow your ideas or plan things in the future. You may use it to brainstorm information (Chapter 5) amongst your team, or you can use them to assign roles and tasks. If the team has a set of tasks it must complete or to assign various roles, the manager can allocate the different tasks or roles to each member of the team.

You can use visual aids to organize your staff members too and if you are assigning more than one role or task, you can use your mind map to prioritize your tasks and put them in a logical order.

You can also use them with your team, as a group exercise. This will give you the ability to problem solve (Chapter 16), grow your business ideas and make business decisions too (Chapter 9).

Setting goals and targets is also important in business. Now we've discussed goal setting several times, and in detail in Chapter 8, remember that mind mapping techniques can be applied to many different situations.

Mind Mapping for Better Sales and Marketing

A business needs a robust sales and marketing strategy, if it wants to succeed and visual maps are great for this. In order to create a mind map for sales and marketing, you need to think about if you are wanting to market the business as a whole or if you have a product or service in mind.

If you are wanting to market the business in general, your central idea is the actual marketing of your business. You can then branch off into subcategories. You should consider the unique selling points of the business, the customer (think about what your customer wants), the benefits of your business or product, and you should discuss how you can solve your customer's problems. After that, you can focus on what methods of marketing you could use to reach that ideal customer of yours and you should also list your different products and services, as well as sales targets for each of these. You can then make a more in-depth strategy considering how you can serve your customer and why they would choose you. You should also think about how many of each product and service you would have to sell in order to achieve your sales target.

If you want to create a focused sales and marketing strategy based on a particular product or service, then you can go more in-depth with this. In this instance, your product or service should be your central idea. You can then create goals for this product or service, indicate your ideal customer for this product or service and develop financial strategies for this. You should also consider where your customer is and how can you reach them. You need to know this in order to work out your best method of advertising. Once you list your methods of advertising, list them in order of importance and you can even attach a cost, as this enables you to work out overall expenditure. This will be great for budgeting purposes!

Remember that sales and marketing strategies need to concentrate on your customer and should sell the benefits of your company, product or service. You should do your research and listen to your customer, A single method of marketing is likely not to be effective, so ensure you use many different marketing strategies and if you're posting or advertising online, you need to be regular and consistent.

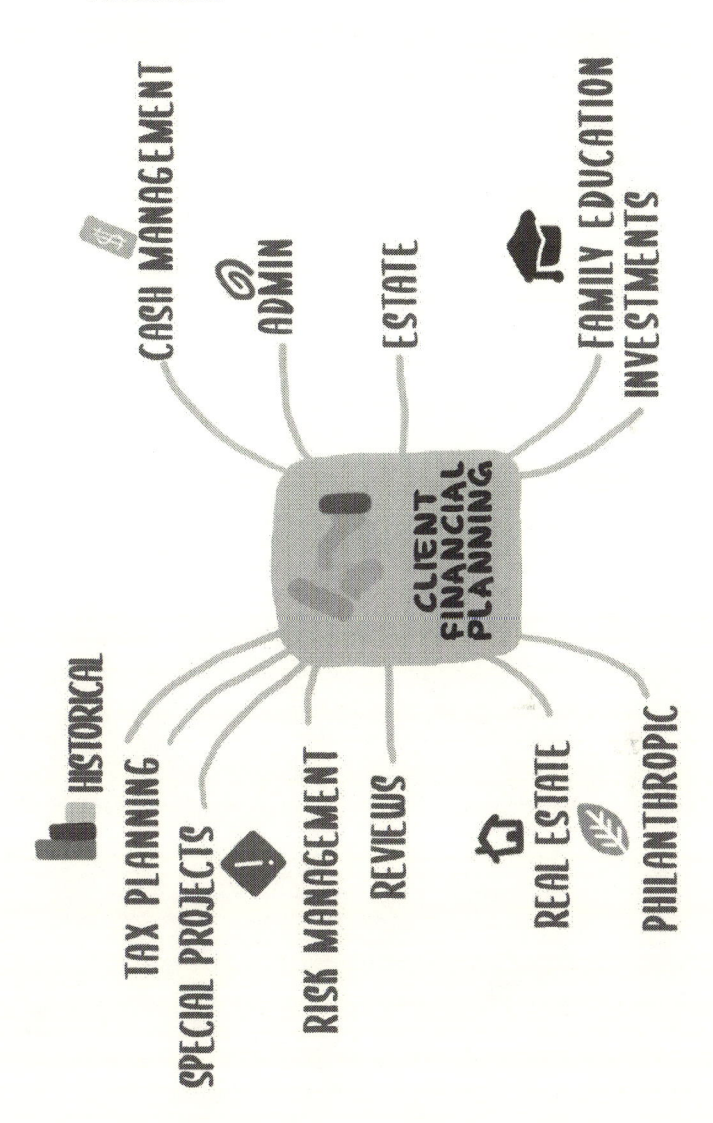

CLIENT FINANCIAL PLANNING
- CASH MANAGEMENT
- ADMIN
- ESTATE
- FAMILY EDUCATION
- INVESTMENTS
- PHILANTHROPIC
- REAL ESTATE
- REVIEWS
- RISK MANAGEMENT
- SPECIAL PROJECTS
- TAX PLANNING
- HISTORICAL

Mind Mapping for a Meeting

Mind mapping is great if you're planning or hosting a meeting. To start with, you can use mind mapping techniques for your notetaking at a meeting (Chapter 7 and 10 are useful in relation to notetaking). Earlier in this chapter we talked about visual mapping techniques when presenting and there are times when we might have to present information at a meeting. The different chapters we've already explored in this book are great if you want to create mind maps for a meeting.

Mind maps can also be used when you're planning a meeting too, and they can help you to host a well-organized meeting. If you want to use mind mapping for the planning stages, you should think about your end goal, the items/subjects you want to discuss, your attendees, any equipment you need and the basic meeting information. From this, you should be able to create a to-do list for arranging the meeting and your agenda.

Mind Mapping for a Meeting

who
- atendees: CEO, Gwen, Rhodi, Shahid
- contact: Company ABC, Company XYZ
- organise: Venue, Supplies, Follow up

agenda
- welcome: breakfast meeting, XYZ Company
- business: items
- action
- breaks: 10 AM

when
- date: 2nd December
- time: 8:30 AM
- duration: 3 hrs

location
- head office

objectives
- creative brief: explore
- ideas: generate
- proposal: define
- project plan: begin

supplies
- food: fruit, Danish pastries
- drink: tea, iced water, coffee
- material: mind map, noting
- equipment: AV, laptop, speakers

meeting Plan

167

Mind Mapping for Interviews

If you conduct interviews at work, mind mapping can be a great tool to form your interview questions. Before you begin, you may need to do a little research into the role you are interviewing. For example, you might need to know, *what experience are the applicants will need? What qualifications do they need? What are key roles and responsibilities of this role?*

Write out the name of the job role that you are interviewing for in the center, as this is your central idea. Visualize the job role and use your branches to brainstorm interview questions that you need to ask.

When you've done this, analyze your questions against the job description, the role specification and the key roles and responsibilities of that job. Link your questions to elements of these documents by using key words that link the questions and requirements of the role. *Is there anything you haven't covered in your questioning?* You can add notes or extra questions at this point.

You can now form your interview questions and you will know how to assess the person you are interviewing easily.

15

Mind Mapping your Business Idea

If you have not yet started your business or if you want to expand your business and have an idea, mind mapping can be an innovative way for you to plan your business and its growth. You can brainstorm ideas, form a business model and produce growth strategies.

Start with your Business Idea

To plan your business idea in its initial phase you would use brainstorming strategies discussed in Chapter 5 and apply them to your business idea. Before you begin, you should use questions to ensure you know the relevant information about your business and your idea. You can form your own questions, but if you don't know where to start, check out the questions below and adapt them to suit your own needs.

For example:

- What products and services will my business offer and what makes me different?
- Who is my customer and who is my competition?
- Where is my business located?
- When do I want to launch my business?
- Why will my business succeed?
- How will my business succeed?

> **A Quick Note**
>
> Create your brainstorm around these questions but go deeper. Your idea itself should be the central focus, but then you should branch off to note down your ideas. You don't need to know the answers in detail, but there are some of the things you should be thinking about. Once you know the basis of your business, your brainstorming session is more likely to work in your favour because your creative and innovative ideas will flow, so use key words from your subcategories to expand on your ideas further. This will enable you to organise your thoughts and form a strong plan.

When you have a solid idea, you can make a business plan around this. You should set business goals and you can use mind maps to come up with these. You can also use mind maps to brainstorm names for your business too, if you don't have one already.

Financials ← Exectutive Summary ↗

Strategy ←

Company ↘

Management Team ↙ **Business Plan** ↘ Market

↙ Products

How to Form a Business Model Using Mind Maps

A business idea needs to be explored in-depth and in a specific way, but a business model is overview of your business as a whole and can help you to plan the financial aspects too. You should have an ideal monthly earning figure in mind when you create your model so just briefly think about what your ideal earning sum is. Obviously, you may need to think about expenditure of the business too.

Your central idea can be something as simple as *My Business Idea,* or the name of your business if you have one already. You can then start to brainstorm your business and you can tailor your diagram to suit your own needs – for instance, maybe you need to invest money, or you could need equipment.

The products and services are the leading aspect of your business, so from your central idea, you need to branch off and 3-5 key products or services you want to offer as part of your business. These will form your subcategories. From this, you should then think about what income you need to bring in from each product/service. Set yourself income goals and think about the cost of these products and services:

How much investment will it take to provide the product or service?

What is the cost per unit?

How many do you need to sell to hit your target?

Product / Service 1

Product / Service 2

MY BUSINESS

Product / Service 5

Product / Service 4

Product / Service 3

You have now begun to build a model for your business but as discussed earlier, you do need to go a little more in depth. Explore what your unique selling points are and assess when you can offer or launch this product or service. Marketing is also important, but you can check out Chapter 14 for that.

You can use the information from your brainstorming session and your business model when completing your business plan. Once you have envisioned the whole picture, have income goals and know your products and services that will appeal to your customer, you have the information you need to produce your business plan.

Don't sell yourself short and keep pushing forward with your ideas. Break down each product and services and think how many hours each week you will have to commit to each. Make sure you apply your mind map to your business as your model, it's structure and content will all contribute to effective planning.

For your business plan to be viable you should test yourself and ask yourself – *what makes my business/product/service different? How will I compete? Why will people choose me?* You should also make sure that you are clear on your ideal customer and everything should be tailored towards that specific customer.

Having a plan for future growth is also a great way to push the boundaries of your business and demonstrate that you are in it for the long-term. Your business plan can spell out the first 12 months of your business, but you should push yourself even further and create a 5-year growth plan.

Where do you see yourself/your business in five years?

Growing your Business Idea

We should all have future goals for our business and because visual maps are great for brainstorming, you can use this concept to grow your business idea. If you are in business are planning to start one, you can use mind maps for growth purposes. Visualize your business and think about its future.

What do you want to happen?

What future goals do you have?

What do you visualize for your business?

Review your products and services that you offer now, or plan on offering. Ask yourself, *how can I take these to the next level?*

You may find that some of your products and services sell better than others. This could impact your future decisions as you may offer more of a specific product or service than another. For example, you may decide to get rid of one low-performing product or service, but it may not be the one you expected it to be. You may also decide to do some customer research, as you need to know what your customer wants moving forward, and what their plans are for the future.

Another thing to consider is that business growth can mean you need to take on new members of staff or outsource some of your tasks so you can work on the more profitable aspects of the business. Sometimes plans change, but don't worry, mind maps are flexible.

Review the products or services that you currently offer or plan to offer and note them down on branches coming from your central idea (business growth). Then, from these subcategories, branch our further and name one way that you can grow this specific product/service. For example, if you coach or train on a one-to-one basis, you could make the transition from one-to-one, to small group work. The price per person will be lower, but the amount of people that require that particular service will increase.

You should then visualize your business and think about at least one extra product or service you might like to offer in the future. Remember to cost everything up, so that a lucrative strategy for growth can be put together. Also think about costs, for instance if you need to employ members of staff/outsource, the business costs will increase.

Don't be afraid to do your research and make any necessary amendments. Find out what other similar businesses are doing, think about how you can make that work for your business and how you can make your product or service different.

Sell your products and services by highlighting the benefits and unique selling points of your products or services.

Often, mind maps that focus on business models, plans and growth can be very motivating. Don't forget to always use your business-related mind map to construct SMART goals and objectives that will help you achieve your business hopes and dreams.

16

Mind Mapping for Problem Solving

Problem solving has been discussed in previous chapters, but *how can we use mind maps to solve problems?* The truth is, once you are familiar with mind mapping techniques, it's not difficult to put this into practice for almost any situation. If you have a topic in mind, but there are problems or issues that you need to address you can use these techniques and you can also use them to diagnose problems too.

How to Find Solutions & Answers

Write your central idea or goal in the center of your diagram and visualize what you are trying to achieve. Take a few seconds to think about the barriers that are stopping you from achieving this. You can then start to brainstorm the problems that you need to address.

Once you have created your mind map of problems, you can then study your mind map. Use a color code to identify minor problems that can be solved easily and another color to identify major problems.

First, you should address your minor problems. They should be problems that you can resolve yourself, easily. They will be easily rectified, and you probably won't have to think too much about how to resolve the issues. Start to use twigs and key words to demonstrate how you can resolve each of your easily solved problems.

Problem
- Define
- Gather Opinions
- Explore

Solutions
- Result

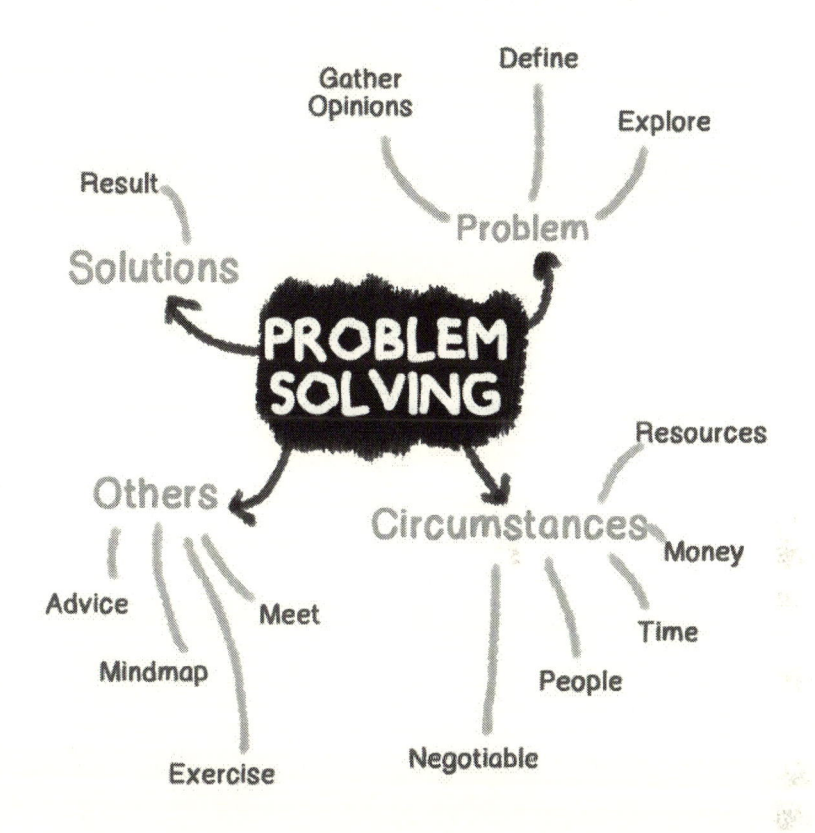

Others
- Advice
- Meet
- Mindmap
- Exercise

Circumstances
- Resources
- Money
- Time
- People
- Negotiable

For any major problems you may encounter, you will need to think about these carefully. If a problem is more complex, it's important to address this in a professional but effective way. This means you need to think more strategically. If you are in business or work for a company, you can address your major issues by:

- Speaking to other colleagues (brainstorming meetings).

- Asking a manager or expert for advice.
- In some cases, it's appropriate to communicate with your customers.
- Research is also important for a positive outcome.

Showing you have a plan of action when addressing barriers or problems demonstrates a forward-thinking attitude. As human beings we are natural problem solvers who will not give up, simply because there are obstacles in our way.

Sometimes, there are barriers that aren't clear to us but don't worry, mind maps can be used to diagnose problems too.

How to Diagnose Problems

Do you remember when that thing you were doing did not go according to plan? Something stops you in your tracks but you're not quite sure what it is or why it's happening?

If this is happening or has happened to you, visual maps could be the answer. Until we know what the problem is, we can't be expected to find a realistic solution.

IT issues are common. Often IT malfunctions and it could be as a result of numerous reasons, so you have to eliminate possibilities in order to arrive at the actual problem. Only then can you resolve the issue.

Now let's use an 8-step process to demonstrate how we can diagnose problems effectively.

1. The first step is to write your problem down in the center of your diagram in as few words as possible.
2. You should then identify possible causes of problems. Now usually, it is recommended that you use free and creative thinking when mind mapping, but if you are unfamiliar with the topic, you may need to research information. In this case you can use your visual aid to identify possible problems or issues. Just note them down as a subcategory.
3. Read the definitions of the possible problem causes if you are not familiar with them already and use twigs with associated key words that will prompt you in identifying this type of problems (what are the signs and symptoms of this problem?).
4. When you have many possibilities, you should visualize your problem. Think about

what signs and symptoms are showing and compare them to the problem causes.
5. If you are drawing a blank right now, don't be afraid to return to your original map and complete further research. Consult with experts or your team if need be and ask them, what they think the biggest problem is and why. Again, you could consult your customer.
6. You can then start the elimination process. Start to analyze the possible problems in-depth and compare your problem to this diagnostic. If it doesn't match, then strike it from your mind map. If it does match and this could still be causing the problem, use a color code to identify that this is a possible problematic area.
7. When you have eliminated as many of the likely problems as possible and you are left with only a few (or even one) problem cause, you can use your visual map to form a diagnostic checklist. Think about what you must do in order to confirm that it is this specific issue that is causing your problem and think about how you can resolve your problem.
8. Use the checklist as a diagnostic tool and follow it until you are satisfied that your problem is resolved.

Of course, there are occasions when you can't find the answer and may need to look elsewhere or gain a professional opinion in order to resolve a complex issue. This is something that we should accept, especially if we do not specialize in that area. In that case, we should use our newly found knowledge to learn. Our problem-solving abilities are transferable skills that we can apply to many situations and as we learn and develop our skills, we grow.

This leads us nicely onto the next chapter of how we can use mind maps to learn new languages.

17

Mind Mapping for Learning New Languages

There's no doubt that learning a new language is great for development and growth. As we learn, we challenge ourselves and keep our brain active. Learning a new language is not always easy, especially when we know and understand the grammar rules of our mother-tongue.

Mind mapping is useful if we want to learn. Language acquisition usually occurs at a young age for our first language, but bilingual people certainly exist. If we can learn in the right way, then we can learn new languages quickly and effectively.

Visual maps can certainly assist with this type of learning and we will discuss in-depth, in the sections to follow.

Using Mind Maps for Learning

It's a proven fact that images are great learning resources. They can help us to absorb and store information in our memory. We've talked about visual maps extensively and techniques like brainstorming and notetaking which are also useful when learning. Here are three top tips of how you can use mind maps for effective learning, with maximum impact:

1. Be as creative as possible; mind mapping should be fun, and it should allow you to think freely and creatively. Use colors, shapes and images to make your map as visually appealing and memorable as possible.
2. The way you present the information is important. Use subcategories to group together specific, related information. Your mind map should be in a logical order that you can make sense of. You can use images to represent your groups and/or use different colors for each word group so that you can see the link visually.

3. Don't be afraid to adapt your diagram, make additions and add notes. Make sure that the mind map is organized in a way that suits you. It should be unique, and you should be able to make sense of it. [20]

How to Organize Your Words When Learning a New Language

If you are learning a new language, you need to organize your words in a way that you will understand. Visuals enable us to organize information effectively in our brain and memory, which in turn helps us learn and comprehend information by making links thinks that are familiar to us.

When we start to learn our mother- tongue at a young age, we use flashcards to create word-picture links. As we are already well versed in our first language now, we could have a topic in the center and words associated with that topic. For instance, if English is your first language, you could have an English word or a related picture, noted next to its equivalent in another language. We could even make a phonics link in brackets, that tells us how to pronounce the word sounds easily. See the image below:

- Vasiselle
- Lassive
- Cuisine
- Babysitting
- des courses

Faire

Balauer

Passer

Je Dois

Tondre

Debarrasser

Ranger

Table La

La Vaiselle
Ma Chambre

Mettre

Couvert Le

Preparer

Sortir

Laver

Poubelle La

Les Repas

Voiture La

If you have a more in-depth knowledge of the language and need to explore sentence patterns or grammar rules, visual maps can really help you put this information into perspective. We've already discussed ways to use mind maps for effective study in Chapter 7, and here is an example of how that can be displayed below:

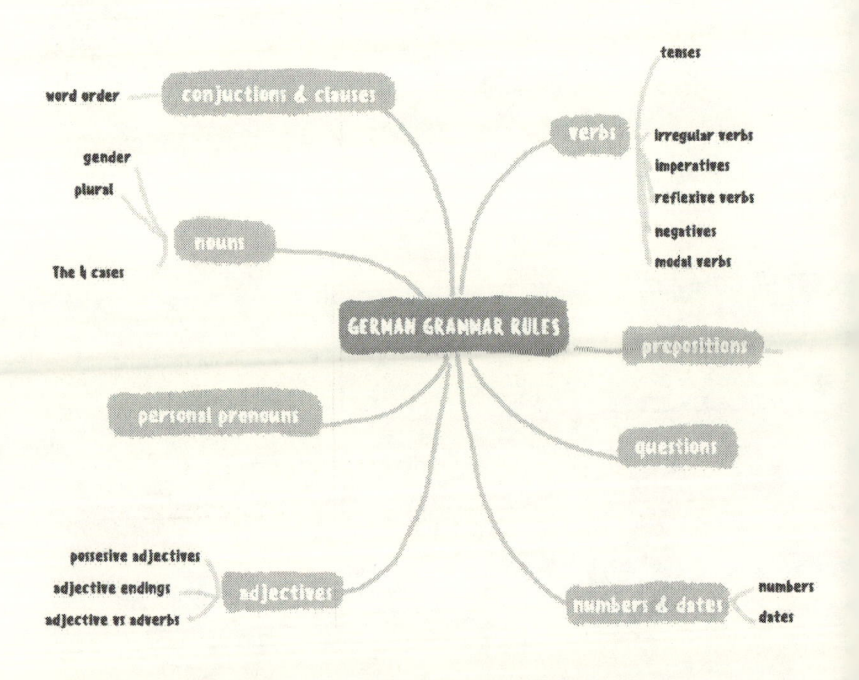

```
                                                    tenses
word order — conjuctions & clauses
                                          verbs    irregular verbs
     gender                                        imperatives
     plural                                        reflexive verbs
                        nouns                      negatives
The 4 cases                                        modal verbs

                    GERMAN GRAMMAR RULES
                                            prepositions

              personal pronouns
                                            questions

possesive adjectives
adjective endings    adjectives                              numbers
adjective vs adverbs                    numbers & dates      dates
```

Now as you can see, the mind map will act, not only to help us visualize and learn the grammar rules, but it also acts as a great study tool for revision purposes.

The way we order our words is important too. If we can make a connection to something we already know, it becomes easier to learn and remember the words. When we learn the days of the week, we can sing the words to the *Days of the Week* song that we learned, when we first started school. This is because we learn through patterns and sounds, as well as imagery.

Think about the order we say the days of the week for a moment and imagine that we are currently learning French days, months and numbers...

If we list words like this:

Days – Lundi, Mardi, Mecredi...

We would automatically remember that they are Monday, Tuesday and Wednesday in French, because of their word order. The word order stays the same, even though the words are different.

How to Compare Languages

We talked in the last section about noting down a word in our mother-tongue or using an associated picture, followed by the word equivalent in the language we are learning, and mind maps are great when comparing. They can be used to review the similarities and differences. When we compare something, we look at one thing against another (sometimes more than one other thing), so this means you should split your visual map into mirroring sections.

For example, if we refer to a French example again, we could compare English words to their French equivalents, or if you are working at a complex level, you could compare the grammar rules (with examples).

It's always good to compare sentence structures when studying another language too, as the components used in a clause or sentence structure can differ. Comparing these in a visual way can really help us to comprehend differences.

How to Compare Languages

French to English

French Days & Months

Days of the Week

English	French
Monday	lundi
Tuesday	mardi
Wednesday	mercredi
Thursday	jeudi
Friday	vendredi
Saturday	samedi
Sunday	dimanche

Months of the year

English	French
January	janvier
February	février
March	mars
April	avril
May	mai
June	juin
July	juillet
August	aout

18

Mind Mapping for Everyday Life

If you love mind maps, it will please you to know that you can use them for everyday tasks. *That's right,* you can use them to plan gifts, to write your shopping list, for gift ideas, to plan a wedding or to plan your networking. You can even plan your exercise routine or health and fitness in general.

Check out some of the most common ways to use mind maps throughout this section and see if you can think of your own use for them too.

Networking

We can use mind maps to plan, make the most of, or even limit our networking usage. The principles are the same really because your central idea is to network. If you are doing this for business or for something you are doing personally, you should think about what your goal is. For example, a business might want to build an audience, whereas someone who thinks they spend too much time on Facebook might want to limit or reduce their social media usage and increase personal, face to face, networking groups.

You should then write the different networking groups that you want to tap into. So, for instance, maybe a person who is self-employed wants to attend specific networking groups in their area and is signing up to networking meetings. Maybe they also want to spend 1-2 hours per day, building up an online audience too.

Therefore, they would want to mix-up their networking. People network for many reasons and sometimes this could be to make friends, to learn something, or because you have something in common and would like to build up contacts.

Shopping for Gifts

If you are shopping for gifts, mind maps are perfect. If it's a person's birthday, then you might put their name in the center (central idea) and then list all the gifts you think the person would like. You could then use a process of elimination to confirm your choice. This would be in the essence of a brainstorm to grow your ideas.

If it's a special occasion like Thanksgiving or Christmas, then maybe you would name the occasion in the center, and then your subcategories could be the names of all the people you need to buy gifts for. You can then use your twigs, colors, shapes, and maybe images to highlight gift ideas. If you are not sure, maybe you could link up to that person's hobbies or interests, so that you can think further about what the perfect gift would be each specific person.

You can even use a mind map to give other people gift ideas too. *Have you ever been invited to a birthday party, christening or wedding and you don't know what to buy as a gift?* In the next section we will talk about planning a wedding. Many people who plan a wedding have a wedding gift list to give their attendees gift ideas.

Planning a Wedding

If you are planning a significant event, such as a wedding, there is so much to think about. Visual maps can be very useful as they can help you to create a to-do list and consider costs too.

Look at the diagram below to see the different things you might have to think about if you are planning your wedding:

How to Plan a Wedding

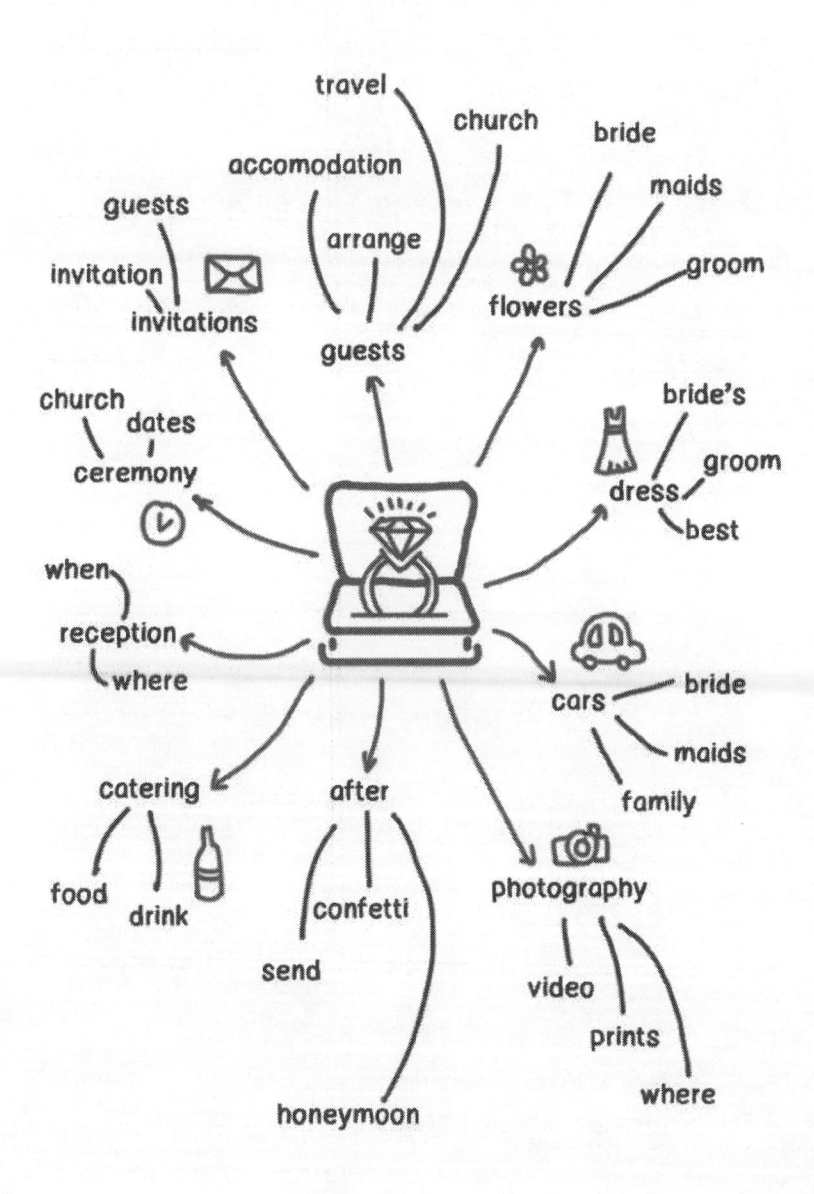

- guests
  - invitation
  - invitations

- travel
- accomodation
- arrange
- guests

- church
- bride
- maids
- groom
- flowers

- church
- dates
- ceremony
- when
- reception
- where

- bride's
- groom
- dress
- best

- cars
  - bride
  - maids
  - family

- catering
  - food
  - drink

- after
  - confetti
  - send
  - honeymoon

- photography
  - video
  - prints
  - where

198

You can go further with your mind map, once you've completed the initial phase. For instance, we all know that weddings require a venue, but it's not as simple as just choosing and booking a venue. If you are planning your wedding, one of your subcategories would be venue, but then from this, you would have a list of possible venues that you are interested in. Once you've viewed them you could detail the cost and use colors to represent how you felt about the venue – pink for *it's the one* green for good, amber for okay and red for no way! You could then make a folder of your favorite venues with information about the package they will offer you.

For subjects such as venues, you may need to create a mind map, that sums each of them up, so that you can make an informed decision and comparison of venues. If you're getting married, then it's your special day so you need to make the right decision.

Meal Planning and Food Shopping List

You can use visuals to plan your meals for the week, and your shopping list. To do this you should note down your central idea, which in this case are your weekly meals. The subcategories should be the days of the week and then the twigs can indicate breakfast, lunch, dinner and snacks.

When you've completed this initial stage, you can go back to each day and note down what food you require for each day, so you know what food you need to buy this week. Don't forget to include drinks too.

You can then form your shopping list based on your mind map.

Health and fitness

You can use visual maps to create, plan and monitor your own health and fitness. You must consider this topic carefully, because health and fitness are customized based on your needs and expectations. Your map will always be individual to you, because it depends how you interpret the idea of being fit and healthy, and how you choose to approach this. Your goal will be different to others, because it's your individual plan.

If you have a goal to lose weight, or you want to create your own health and fitness regime, then you should certainly turn to mind maps. You could even use your mind map to plan out your own healthy meals

Check out the diagram below to see how you can plan your own health and fitness:

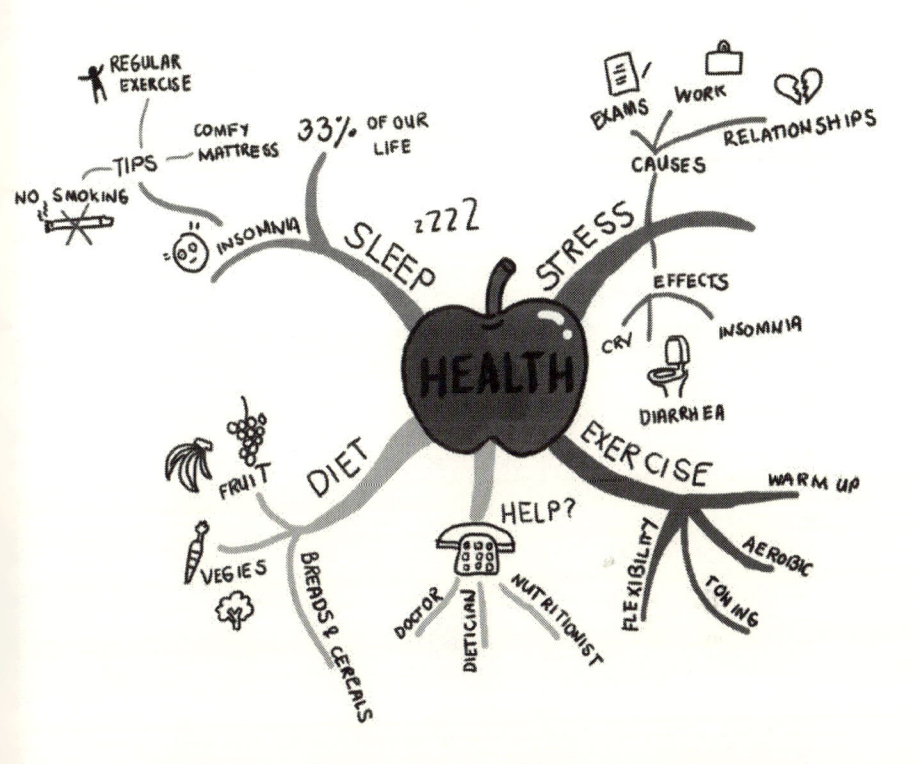

Before you begin, you could have a weight goal in mind. Turn this into a SMART goal and list all the things you need to do, to hit your target. For instance, exercise, meals, meditation, *how often will you get weighed/measured? What exercise routine will you*

follow? What diet are you following? You should then think about how you can manage your cravings, how you will stay motivated and how can you maximize results.

A great benefit of a visual map is its flexibility. If you have a fitness/exercise regime, you can start to increase the difficulty level, as you progress, increase your fitness level and start to lose weight. Start adding some new exercises, when it's no longer challenging.

You can also think about what you need to do to stay healthy. Our BMI (body mass index) is calculated based on our age, sex and height, so our dietary requirements and calorie/fat intake differs. It's important to reflect on what health is for you. We talk a lot about having a healthy diet, and regular exercise but we also need to have a healthy mind too. Spending time meditating or reading your affirmations might be just as important to ensure you are of sound mind.

Be true to your mind, body and soul!

19

Mind Mapping with Children

Mind maps can really help us to learn and express our ideas. They are also great for children too as mind mapping comes naturally to us. The whole process is fun, yet it teaches children to think creatively, get information onto a page, and organize their thoughts and ideas. Children are the epitome of imagination, so they can have fun while they are learning. If this skill is embedded from a young age, it can have endless benefits to a child's learning and development.

Helping Children to Express their Ideas

In the same way that a mind map can help adults to express their ideas in a creative way, mind mapping can be effective for children too.

Creating a visual map can be a fun and ideal way to get children to express their ideas. Children often don't like to feel forced into writing a lot of information down on the page. Children respond well to images, so let them cut and stick pictures, use colors and shapes of their choice and allow them to use key words as prompts.

You can then question the children on their diagram to help them expand their ideas and challenge their knowledge and understanding of a topic.

Ask probing questions that ignite a response – *Who? What? When? Where? Why? How?*

Why Mind Mapping Works for Children

The reason mind mapping works for children is quite simple. When we teach children early, we use pictures to show meanings of words and sounds. Picture-word association is still an effective tool for a child and something that is visually appealing suddenly feels like fun, rather than work.

If we can provide a fun task for children to complete while they are working, they begin to find learning fun, and this is valuable because it instills a positive learning environment.

Children are like a sponge – they take in so much information as they are on a constant learning journey. Mind mapping is the perfect way to help them process the information and make sense of it all.

Make Mind Mapping a Game

Learning games are popular all over world, so if you turn visual maps into a game it can spark a child's interest easily. There are many games you could try that involves mind maps.

Story Retell: You could read a story to your child or children, and then you could give them a visual

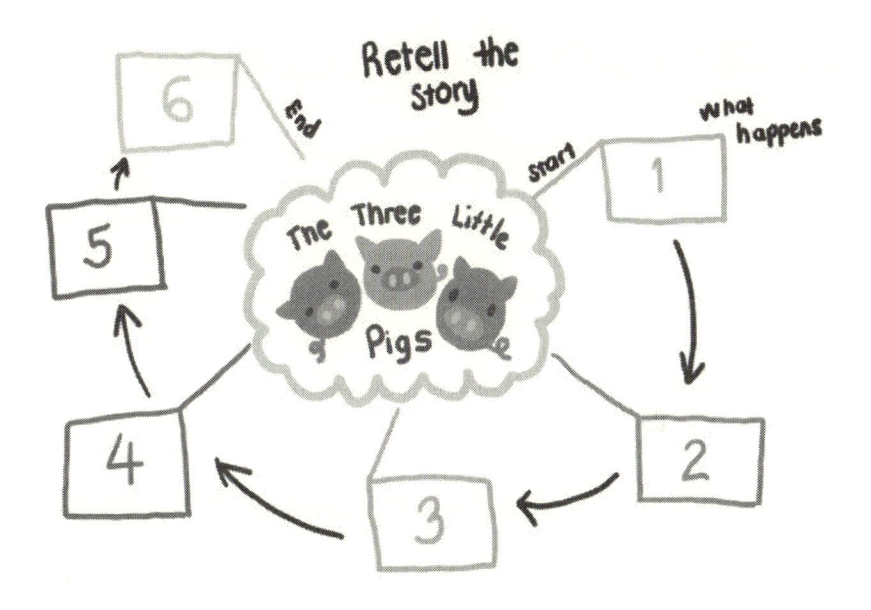

[Diagram: "Retell the story" mind map with numbered boxes 1-6 arranged around a central cloud labelled "The Three Little Pigs". Arrows flow from "start" at box 1, through boxes 2, 3, 4, 5, to "End" at box 6. Label "what happens" near box 1.]

map template that is numbered 1-6. The children are then given pictures and they must stick the story pictures in order within the mind map diagram.

Now this is a very simple exercise so you can make it harder, depending on the age and ability of the child or children. Ask them to use key words to accompany the picture. They could name characters or indicate what happens in each section of the story. They could make notes about the story structure like genre and key themes here too.

You could get them to tell the story using the mind map as a prompt, as the images and/or key words will help to give confidence.

Older children could explore and analyze stories. We'll stay with the theme of *Humpty Dumpty;* see the next image for an example…

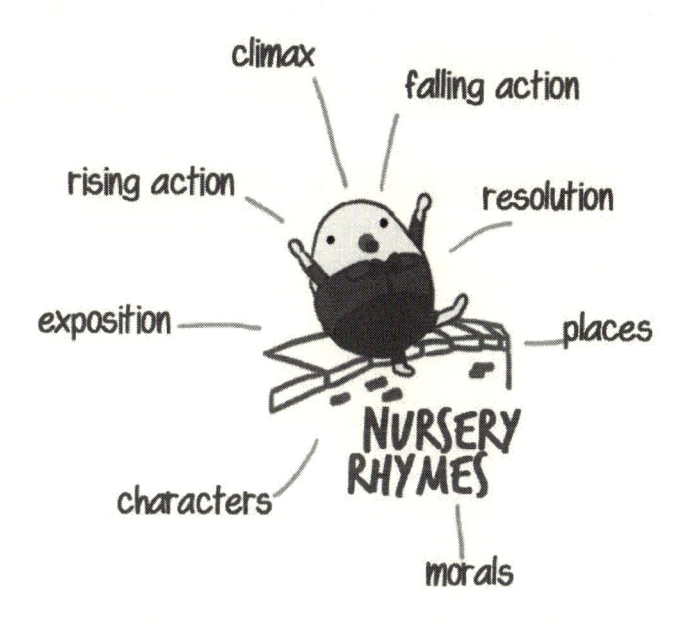

                    climax
    rising action | falling action
         \ | /
          \ | /
                           resolution
    exposition ———   ——— places

                  NURSERY
    characters / RHYMES
                     |
                   morals

Notetaking: Another game is to learn about a topic and take notes using the mind map. You could allow children to think freely and note down anything that they think is a key point from the exercise.

Show and Tell: A child can create a show and tell activity using images in form of a map. They can talk about an interest or something that they've done or enjoyed. They could even make a mind map of their family too.

Timed mind map: A child can either watch a video clip or read a book and afterwards, they can be timed to note as much down on a mind map template as they can remember from memory only.

Critical Thinking Group Exercise: If children have been studying a topic for a longer period of time, they can create a mind map as part of a group and then they can present the information. With group work, everyone should have a role and you'll find that ideas bounce from person to person.

Using a Mind Map to Help Children Learn

Mind maps are great to help children learn. When first starting off with them, you could provide a template and even model how to complete a mind map.

If a child is studying for a test, visual aids are great. You could have the name of the test in the center, followed by the topics covered in the test. For example, for a math's test, you might study 2D shapes, 3D shapes, addition, subtraction, times tables, and also areas and measurement.

A child can then add key words on twigs and use shapes. They can highlight things in a different color that they need to work on further and use the mind map as a kind of revision guide.

Much of what discussed earlier assists with learning. For instance, children could note down things they know about electricity in a timed environment, they could retell a story or put information into a logical order, and they could even use mind maps to note take. Things like spellings and languages can also be learned by using such techniques.

We should also consider how visuals can help us to plan our work too, and this is something that children can embrace. From a young age, children are taught to plan their writing and school projects. This is great because it teaches children to plan ahead, be prepared and think logically.

See how a child could be encouraged to use a mind map to learn about history on the next page.

Visual maps can also be used to plan that art project, or even a recipe too. Stories can also be planned using mind maps, which leads us nicely onto the next section.

How to Teach Children About History

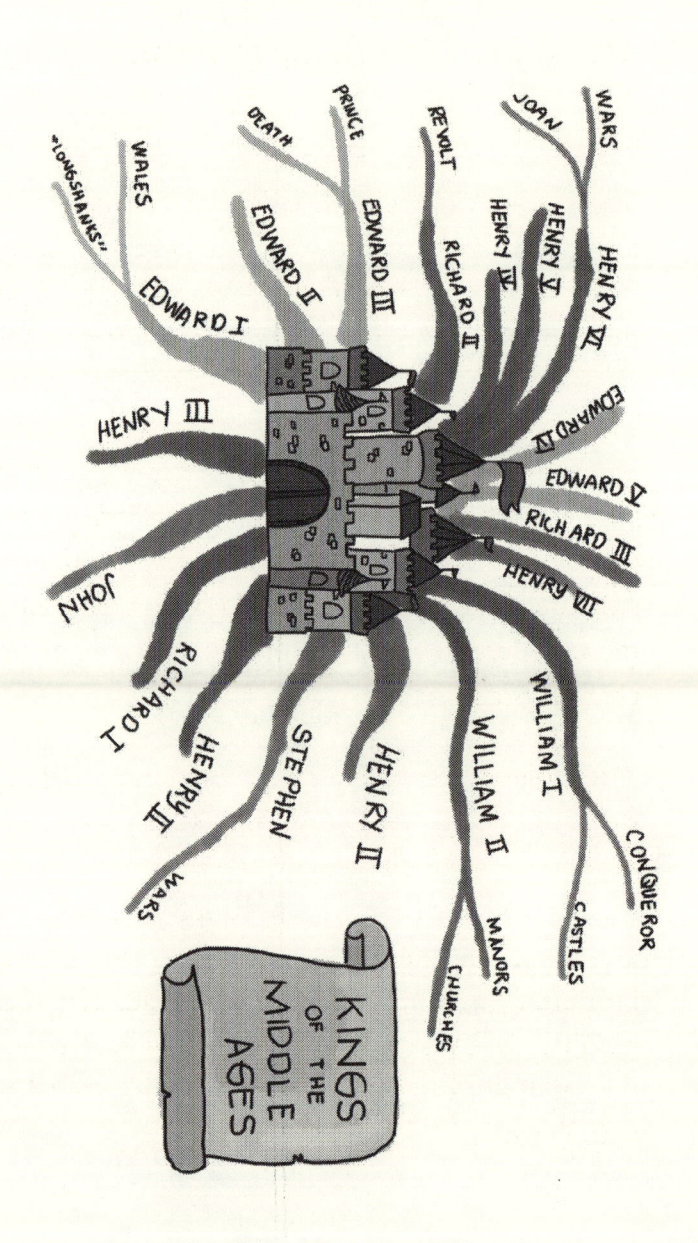

Using Mind Mapping to Form a Story

To plan a story, similar concepts can be used as discussed in Chapter 6. A child can be encouraged to create a mind map to plan and form their story, but it can be tailored to their age and ability. Split the mind map template into two halves. In one half the child can discuss characters, setting and genre. In the second half, three subcategories are needed: beginning, middle and end. The child can then sequence their story. This means that the child can demonstrate creativity, show knowledge of story structure and format, as well as thinking a little more in-depth about the story by exploring genre, characters and setting.

Alternatively, for younger children a brainstorming approach could be great too. You could get the child to use a mind map template and have 6 boxes leading from the center – they should be numbered 1-6. The child could be encouraged to write a story by putting a sentence in each box, starting with number 1. This can teach story structure and format and it can build a child's confidence when writing stories.

The creativity involved with mind mapping is certainly beneficial and is a great way to help a child develop and learn.

20

Group Mind Mapping

Group mind mapping is popular at training events and meetings. Often, if one person has an idea in a group environment and they say it aloud, it inspires another person and they have another idea. Mind mapping in a group needs a facilitator and the facilitator will assist, monitor and support the groups. They might ask questions for instance, to prompt further thinking.

Group Ideas and Ensuring Everyone Counts

If you are facilitating group mind mapping, you need to set some ground rules as in order for this to work. You need to create an environment that makes everyone feel comfortable and respected, but also able to express their ideas and opinions.

Your ground rules might include:

- ✓ Everyone knows what needs to be achieved by the end of the session.
- ✓ Everyone must join in.
- ✓ Every idea is counted: no idea, is a bad idea.
- ✓ We must listen and respect others.

The group facilitator can use questions to prompt discussions and ideas. It's also important for those questions to be directed at attendees on occasions, rather than being open to everyone. If you see that someone isn't joining in as much, you can certainly include them and ask them a question that draws on their opinion or knowledge.

The facilitator is responsible for controlling the session and should strive for maximum results. If the group is managed and facilitated effectively, the session should be insightful and productive.

The Benefits of Group Mind Mapping

Sharing ideas can help a business to grow and its staff to develop. Throughout this book you will have heard that mind maps encourage creative and free thinking. In a group, this can grow on a wider scale because group mind mapping can:

- *Encourage us to think in a different way.* As we all interpret things differently, hearing the opinions and ideas of others can make us rethink the way we do something or view it.
- *Inspire us.* Hearing the ideas and opinions of others can spark further creative thinking and ideas within our own mind.
- *Solve more complex problems.* The more people who come together and work on a problem, the easier it becomes to resolve.
- *Improves communication skills.* Everyone is working together, towards the same goal and this can help to form bonds and an appreciation for one another.
- *Build a deeper understanding of complex tasks.* Looking at every part or component of a process and breaking it down into smaller

parts can really help us to build a stronger understanding.
- **Instills the importance of teamwork** and how important this is in specific environments (like a business environment for instance). [21]

The Drawbacks of Group Mind Mapping

Of course, there are some drawbacks to group mind mapping sessions, but they can be controlled by a skilled facilitator. If you are planning a group session, here are some problems that could occur. You should plan how you could deal with these issues, in advance.

- There could be disagreements of opinion amongst the team as to what is the most important task/product/service is.
- Everyone may not be able to attend.
- If the group is not cooperative or respectful, things won't go as planned.
- If people begin to talk over one another, it becomes difficult to hear any one person's opinion.

- Some people are too shy or anxious to join in.

Good Practices for Group Mind Mapping

If you are facilitating a group session, there are some things you can do to demonstrate good practice:

- ✓ Set ground rules. Why not get your group to take ownership of the rules, by brainstorming them as a group, at the start of your very first meeting/session? Write in the rules that everyone must contribute and reinforce the rule that every idea counts.
- ✓ Include everyone. Give the impression of a supportive environment and ask questions to prompt involvement.
- ✓ Praise creativity.
- ✓ Remind people of the rules.
- ✓ Facilitate effectively, ensuring everyone takes turns, listens and that they don't talk over each other.

- ✓ If a debate gets heated, intervene and calm the situation down. Change the subject or allow a break. Remind everyone of the rules.
- ✓ Teach your students to tap into their creative side by allowing thinking and visualization time.
- ✓ Create a fun, relaxed and open environment.

A good facilitator certainly listens to the group, but they are also fun and approachable. A group mind mapping session can be an effective, innovative tool for developing and growing ideas. The facilitator is important to ensure everything is recorded, everyone is included, and they also ensure that the session moves forward at a steady pace. Their role is to give the best experience and help the group achieve maximum results from their session.

21

Mind Mapping Software

You heard right, there is software available that will create a visual map for you. *Where's the fun in that?* I hear you ask. Well you can still add colors, shapes, curved lines and images, but it's much neater and professional too. If you are a fan of mind maps in a professional capacity, or you don't enjoy the creativity then you should certainly give this a whirl. mind mapping software is fast, accurate and effective and as it does the hard work for you, it will certainly save you time.

Free Software to Create Mind Maps

We've listed our top 6 free mind mapping software for you to check out:

Draw.io is a great mind mapping tool and it's free. This can be used at your desktop, or you can use it on the go. People often get their best ideas when they are on the go.

Coggle is ideal if you're a beginner. There is a free version of this software available. This is for web use only but it's ideal for creating your first mind map. Everyone has to start somewhere.

MindMup is a tool used to create public diagram and if you use this, you can help others through the power of mind maps. There is a free version available.

Mindly is an app that can be downloaded on your smart phone. This is great for those whose mind is most active when they are on the move, and the mobile version is free!

MindMeister is a fantastic mind mapping tool and their basic package is free, but you do have the option to upgrade if you like it.

Stormboard has a free personal plan, if you want to use mind mapping for your personal projects, in everyday life. [22]

22

Beyond Mind Mapping

Mind maps have certainly proved themselves to be a versatile, flexible and effective tool for planning and organizing information in a creative way. In a group, they can embed communication skills and teamwork and they also promote innovation and forward thinking. They encourage us to empty our thoughts onto a page while thinking freely and creatively.

There is very little doubt of their effectiveness as they can motivate and push us to succeed. They help us to make sense of our ideas, thoughts and concepts and develop them further.

We can conclude by clarifying that you now know and understand mind maps, and you can put them into practice... But what's next?

Concepts that are Similar to Mind Maps

There are many concepts to explore that are similar to visual maps. We've named some of these below:

- Process Maps – used to map out standardized processes, usually in a business environment.
- Concept Maps – to help others visualize concepts and ideas. They can help us to comprehend information in a clear way.
- Flow Charts – flow charts are great to help us put actionable steps or procedures in a rational order for us to follow.
- Venn Diagram – Venn diagrams are great comparison tools. They allow us to compare concepts, ideas, things or products, and consider how each are different, but what they have in common too (how are they the same?).
- Fishbone Diagram – usually developed to help us analyze the cause of a specific event. They are often created before a root cause analysis is

produced, to try and solve a problem or work out why there were issues in the first place.

Concise Learning Method (CLM)

Concise Learning Method is a way to improve a learner so that they can accomplish their goals. This is a visual and flexible method, like mind mapping, CLM taps into the cognitive and active mind to help students enhance their memory skills.

According to Tony Krasnik, there are 5 stages to CLM. The 5Ps include preview, participate, process, practice, and produce. [23] Take a look at the following diagram to see how the phases work.

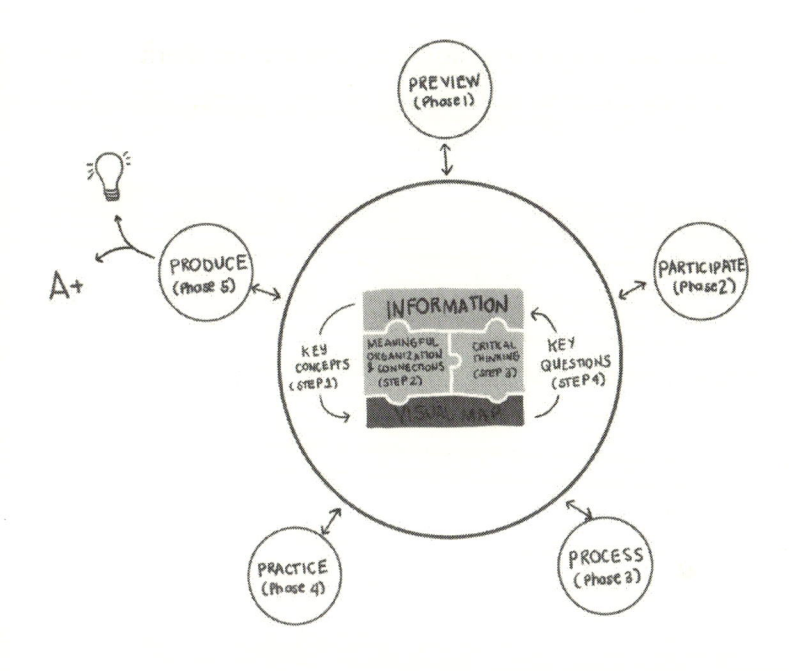

Speed Mind Mapping

In order to mind map quickly, you need to know your topic well and you need to have already had time to process the information too.

If you are manually drawing your mind map, then you need to stick to key words and you should also scrap those colored pens if you want speed. Practice also makes perfect, so you should regularly practice your mind mapping skills too.

Speed mind mapping is something that usually takes place when using software, but this depends on what software you are using. If you want to create a visual map with speed, then you should learn the short cut keys for your program, as this will help you to create your lines, shapes, and assign colors faster.

Conclusion

Congratulations, you've reached the end. You've learnt the secret to mastering mind maps, and how powerful visual mapping can be. *Do you feel good?*

We have uncovered their different uses, different techniques and the various styles and formats that can be used to form your diagrams. Mind maps might not suit everyone, but if you made it to the end of this book, without having made your own yet, then *what are you still doing?* Go make one! They are so much more than a simple image or diagram, because given a chance, they can improve learning, memory and the way we think. They boost creativity and can inspire a whole group of people. If you master mind mapping techniques, it's possible to improve every aspect of your life. They should not be underestimated.

Even if you have used visual maps previously, having a stronger understanding of their true potential can help you get the most from your mind mapping. In this book we have explored the many uses of mind maps and how to create and apply them for maximum results. If goal setting and affirmations help to motivate you, then can certainly benefit from using mind maps in a way that motivates you.

We've looked at the science behind these visuals and considered why they are so innovative. We know that our brain is non-linear, how memories are stored and how our creativity is sparked, and this evidence supports the powerful, positive, impact of the mind map. Take what you've learned from this book and grow, as mind maps will help you to uncover your true potential. The future is bright!

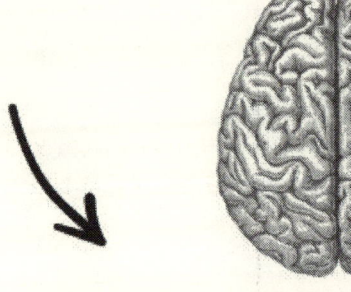

VISIT US ONLINE FOR MORE FREE RESOURCES!

www.thisischarlotte.com/mindmapping

Sign up to receive advance copies, exclusive author templates, discounts and more!

DID YOU ENJOY THIS BOOK?

We would truly appreciate if you could leave a review on Amazon. We are an independent publishing company and read each and every review!

Reference List

[1] Hayes, N. (1994) Foundations of Psychology: An Introductory Text. p.134-135. New York. Routledge.

[2] Buzan, T. and Buzan, B. (1996). The Mind Map Book: How to Use Radiant Thinking to Maximise Your Brain's Untapped Potential. New York: Penguin.

[3] En.wikipedia.org. (2019). Porphyry (philosopher). [online] Available at: https://en.wikipedia.org/wiki/Porphyry_(philosopher) [Accessed 14 Jul. 2019].

[4] History-computer.com. (2019). Ramon Llull - Biography, History and Inventions. [online] Available at: https://history-computer.com/Dreamers/Llull.html [Accessed 23 Jun. 2019].

[5] The Mind Mapping Site. (2019). History of Mind Mapping Basics. [online] Available at:

https://www.mindmappingsite.com/history/history/ [Accessed 9 Jun. 2019].

[6] 6 Cain, M. E. (2001/2002), 'Using Mind Maps to raise standards in literacy, improve confidence and encourage positive attitudes towards learning'. Study conducted at Newchurch Community Primary School, Warrington.

[7] Mind Maps Club. (2019). [online] Available at: http://www.mindmapsclub.com/details2.php?id=40 [Accessed 10 Jun. 2019].

[8] Buzan, T. and Buzan, B. (1996). The Mind Map Book: How to Use Radiant Thinking to Maximise Your Brain's Untapped Potential. New York: Penguin.

[9] Buzan, T. and Buzan, B. (1996). The Mind Map Book: How to Use Radiant Thinking to Maximise Your Brain's Untapped Potential. New York: Penguin.

[10] Vital, M. (2019). 9 Types Of Intelligence - Infographic. [online] Adioma. Available at: https://blog.adioma.com/9-types-of-intelligence-infographic/ [Accessed 5 Aug. 2019].

[11] Niu.edu. (2019). Howard Gardner's Theory of Multiple Intelligences. [online] Available at:

https://www.niu.edu/facdev/_pdf/guide/learning/howard_gardner_theory_multiple_intelligences.pdf [Accessed 23 Aug. 2019].

[12] Niu.edu. (2019). Howard Gardner's Theory of Multiple Intelligences. [online] Available at: https://www.niu.edu/facdev/_pdf/guide/learning/howard_gardner_theory_multiple_intelligences.pdf [Accessed 23 Aug. 2019].

[13] Krasnic, T. (n.d.). [online] Conciselearning.com. Available at: http://www.conciselearning.com/pdf/CLM%20eBook.pdf [Accessed 6 Aug. 2019].

[14] Amir, N. (2019). 10 Ways Nonfiction Authors Can Use Mind Maps to Plan Their Book. [online] Write Nonfiction NOW!. Available at: https://writenonfictionnow.com/10-ways-nonfiction-authors-can-use-mind-maps-plan-book/ [Accessed 7 Jul. 2019].

[15] Gjorgievska, K. (2018). *How does mind mapping help in memorizing?*. [online] Imindq.com. Available at: https://www.imindq.com/blog/how-does-mind-mapping-help-in-memorizing [Accessed 23 Jun. 2019].

[16] Ough, T. (2017). Can't remember names? Always losing keys? Here's how to supercharge

your memory. [online] The Telegraph. Available at: https://www.telegraph.co.uk/health-fitness/mind/cant-remember-names-always-losing-keys-supercharge-memory/ [Accessed 23 Jun. 2019].

[17] En.wikipedia.org. (n.d.). Method of loci. [online] Available at: https://en.wikipedia.org/wiki/Method_of_loci [Accessed 23 Jun. 2019].

[18] En.wikipedia.org. (n.d.). Spaced repetition. [online] Available at: https://en.wikipedia.org/wiki/Spaced_repetition [Accessed 23 Jul. 2019].

[19] En.wikipedia.org. (n.d.). Spaced retrieval. [online] Available at: https://en.wikipedia.org/wiki/Spaced_retrieval [Accessed 23 Jun. 2019].

[20] Jones, T. (2018). 5 Ways to Use a Mind Map As a Learning Tool - Bilingua. [online] Bilingua. Available at: https://bilingua.io/mind-map-as-a-learning-tool [Accessed 23 Jul. 2019].

[21] Brandner, R. (2016). The Teacher's How-To Guide to Group Mind Mapping - Focus. [online] Focus. Available at:

235

https://www.mindmeister.com/blog/group-mind-mapping/ [Accessed 23 Jun. 2019].

[22] Myre, M. (2019). The Best Mind Mapping Software in 2019. [online] Zapier. Available at: https://zapier.com/blog/best-mind-mapping-software/ [Accessed 16 Jul. 2019].

[23] Krasnic, T. (n.d.). [online] Conciselearning.com. Available at: http://www.conciselearning.com/pdf/CLM%20eBook.pdf [Accessed 6 Aug. 2019].

Made in the USA
Monee, IL
15 December 2019